D1479171

PARADOXES OF FAITH

HENRI DE LUBAC

PARADOXES OF FAITH

IGNATIUS PRESS   SAN FRANCISCO

Paradoxes © 1948
Fides Publishers, South Bend, Montreal
Title of the French original: *Paradoxes*
Translated by Paule Simon and Sadie Kreilkamp
© 1945 by Editions du Livre

Further Paradoxes: © 1958
Longmans, Green and Co., Ltd., London
Title of the French original:
Nouveaux Paradoxes
Translated by Ernest Beaumont
© 1955 by Editions du Seuil, Paris

Cover by Victoria Hoke Lane

With ecclesiastical approval
© 1987 Ignatius Press, San Francisco
ISBN 0-89870-132-5
Library of Congress catalogue number 86–62928
Printed in the United States of America

Contents

AUTHOR'S PREFACE

If the expression of a thought is inevitably partial, in the sense that it is incomplete, its elaboration in connected discourse may sometimes mislead and make it appear partial in the other sense of the word. It is hoped that such a risk will in some measure be avoided by a fragmentary presentation. How can fragments be otherwise than incomplete?

Spiritual life and apostolate are often the subject of these fragments. An effort has been made to put aside certain temptations which belong to all ages, but which the present moment has perhaps made more pressing. One imagines that there is no need to make it clear that the writer is not for that reason unaware either of the necessities of temporal action or of the problem it sets the Christian. If it were to be supposed, however, that there were some intention in this little book of making negative criticism, that would be to misjudge the spirit of it. On the contrary, there is the hope that readers may recognize at the back of it a deep sympathy with the immense work of research going on today, in widely differing sectors of the Church, a sympathy that one would have liked to express in more active form.

The very word paradox is paradoxical. Let the paradox be. But how should we define the frequently incomplete reflections of this little book? The reader will decide. In any case, they are not intended to be the discoveries of a solitary mind. Remember, after all, that the Gospel is full of paradoxes, that man is himself a living paradox, and that according to the Fathers of the Church, the Incarnation is the supreme Paradox.

I

Paradox

Paradox is the reverse of what, properly perceived, would be synthesis. But the proper view always eludes us. Each of us contributes by his existence to the weaving of a wonderful tapestry but it cannot yet be comprised entirely within our range of vision. In the field of facts as of spirit, synthesis can only be sought. *Quamdiu vivimus, necesse habemus semper quaerere.*[1] Paradox is the search or wait for synthesis. It is the provisional expression of a view which remains incomplete, but whose orientation is ever towards fulness.

Paradox has more charm than dialectics; it is also more realist and more modest, less tense and less hurried; its function is to remind the dialectician when each new stage is reached in the argument, that however necessary this forward move-

---

[1] "As long as we live, we deem it essential ever to seek."

ment is no real progress has been made. As the scholars of old say, in a rather different sense, of eternal life itself, we are ever going from "beginnings to beginnings".

For paradox exists everywhere in reality, before existing in thought. It is everywhere in permanence. It is for ever reborn. The universe itself, our universe in growth, is paradoxical. The synthesis of the world has not been made. As each truth becomes better known, it opens up a fresh area for paradox. Thought which failed to leave it its place then, which in other words did not recognize this universal place that it has, would be paradoxical in the bad sense. Paradox, in the best sense, is objectivity.

The higher life rises, the richer, the more interior it becomes, the more ground paradox gains. Already sovereign in life that is human only, its realm of election is the life of the spirit. Mystical life is its triumph.

Paradoxes: the word specifies, above all, then, things themselves, not the way of saying them. If it happens as well to bear some subsidiary reflex meaning, perhaps that is indicative of the anxiety to avoid a certain doctrinal heaviness when serious things are being dealt with.

Oppositions in thought express the contradiction which is the very stuff of creation, which permits the movement of history, and which it is the end of this movement to surmount—without ever quite achieving the endeavor.

There are paradoxes of mere expression: one exaggerates in order to emphasize. And there are real paradoxes. These suppose an antinomy: one truth upsets us, another truth balances it. The second truth does not restrict the first, but only places it in the proper perspective. It will not lead us to say "So it was only that." For paradoxical truth is not limited to one plane. That is why, most of the time, neither Christ nor Saint Paul explained a paradox. They feared a foolish interpretation less than one which would debase the truth and deprive it of its "heroism".

Paradoxes are paradoxical: they make sport of the usual and reasonable rule of not being allowed to be *against* as well as *for.* Yet, unlike dialectics, they do not involve the clever turning of *for* into *against*. Neither are they only a conditioning of the one by the other. They are the simultaneity of the one and the other. They are even something more—lacking which, moreover, they would only be vulgar contradiction. They do not sin against logic, whose laws remain inviolable: but they escape its domain. They are the *for* fed by the *against*, the *against* going so far as to identify itself with the *for*; each of them moving into the other, without letting itself be abolished by it and continuing to oppose the other, but so as to give it vigor.

Such is, if you want an example, the paradox of Purgatory. Not only is the soul suffering in Purgatory joyful, but its suffering makes its joy. The absinth of suffering is sweet to the soul:

> . . . *Si tosto m'ha condotto*
> *A ber lo dolce assenzio de'martiri*
> *La Nella mia col suo pianger diretto.*[2]

The only joy with which the joy of Purgatory may be compared is the joy of the blessed in Paradise. St Catherine of Genoa says so after

[2] " . . . So soon has my Nella, by her flood of tears, led me to drink the sweet wormwood of the torments . . ." (Dante, *Purgatorio,* xxiii. 85–7). It is Forese Donati explaining to Dante that it is the merits of the widow he has left on earth which have secured his rising thus far on the Mount of Purgatory.

Dante, and one feels that this view, which is so deep a dogmatic issue, is at the same time the fruit of deep experience: "These souls endure their sufferings so willingly that they would not remove the least atom from them. . . . The excess of their joy does not take away the smallest part of their suffering, nor the excess of their suffering the smallest part of their joy. . . . I do not believe that any contentment may be found comparable with this, except that which the saints in Paradise feel." Anyone who saw in that any trace of a sorrow cult or a too subtle refinement, would show that he has not yet explored his own soul.

The Gospel is full of paradoxes, by which the mind is at first troubled. The Savior teaches with great simplicity, yet he says also, "Blessed is he that shall not be scandalized in me." And it is a question, at least, whether all substantial spiritual doctrine must not of necessity take a paradoxical form.

There is, says Ecclesiastes, a time to speak and a time to be silent. There is a time to support a thesis and a time to enhance the complementary thesis. Moreover it would often seem to be necessary to support them both together, at the same time.

Paradoxical in its substance, spiritual truth is also paradoxical in its rhythm. When we discover it and hold it in our hands we do not have time to bring our first look of satisfaction to rest upon it before it has already fled. The eternal story of the Pharisee starts afresh in each of us. To get hold of this elusive truth again, we should perhaps seek it in its opposite, for it has changed its sign. But often we prefer to hug its rotten corpse. And we go rotten with it.

Decadence, instability, disintegration, corruption, reversal of attitude, all that arises through the simple fact of one's going on existing without self-criticism, self-renewal, constant self-adaptation, without letting anything in one die; through the simple fact of gradually settling down in the vantage point one occupies, the good conscience one enjoys. Such is the permanent danger of all spiritual life. It is an inevitable deterioration which can only be overcome—and painfully at that—by a watchful mustering of strength—unless it be effortlessly vanquished, in a few exceptional cases, by a wonderful gift of grace. . . .

Whence the necessity of paradox: or rather the perpetual flavor of paradox that truth has, when it is freshly expressed, for the man who clings to a truth when it is in the process of turning into a lie.

We are too desirous of being set at ease, and we do not consent to being taken out of our usual element. That is why we make a petty religion for ourselves and seek a petty salvation of our own petty proportions. The Gospel paradoxes are wine too strong for us, and we keep our ears closed to the great liberating Call. We are lacking in courage before all the forms of death which are the necessary gates of Life. In our wretched timidity, we leave the freshness and freedom of Christianity in the hands of those who corrupt them, and even that is a pretext for us to move farther away from Christianity. Encrusted in it like parasites, but with no transforming growth grafted in us from it, we pervert it in the eyes of those for whom we represent it. Making it serve pre-eminently natural man, we take away from it its greatest attraction and cause it to blaspheme.

Such is the history of every century. Such is, O God, we confess, our own everyday history.

Yet how is it, wonder of wonders, that a little light goes on filtering through?

II

Christianity

One deed alone where the living Gospel asserts itself is sufficient to justify the Gospel for ever.

Just as the act of faith is the freest of all acts, so the expression of faith is the most personal of all expressions.

Submissiveness to revealed truth and the supernatural neither prevents us nor dispenses us from receiving these within ourselves so as to express them through ourselves. We escape this interpreter only to fall into banality and verbalism.

17

"Pure faith" or "bare faith" must not be confused with the parroting of a purely literal belief, not truly informed by the mind. The latter is wholly exterior, whereas the former reaches the secret depths of the soul.

Faith is surrender. The believer does not have to encumber himself with theories. Should he make use of them, nothing better. If he wants to reflect on his faith, theories are indispensable to him. He wants them sound and true. But he should keep himself from remaining attached to them as to the own good of his intellect. Faith must share the privilege of charity: it does not seek to lay hold of its object, to monopolize it; it pours forth in it.

Faith does not offer us a theory more beautiful than the philosophers': it raises us above theories. It has us breaking their circles. It makes us escape the limits of our own minds. It carries us past all sublime views on God to God himself. It establishes us in Being. Now this, which alone matters, only faith can do.

The spirit of childhood is a marvellous grace, and it should forever be repeated with the Gospel that the Kingdom of Heaven is for children and for those who resemble them. But the spirit of childhood is different from puerility, spiritual candor is quite another thing from intellectual weakness, and Saint Paul also must be listened to when he says: *Evacuavi quae erant parvuli.* The Church is a mother: now, says Saint Augustine, a mother loves to feed her little child, but she does not want him to remain a little child indefinitely. (Sermon 23: *et mater parvulum amat nutrire, sed eum non amat parvulum remanere.*)

We fool ourselves if we think that by denying the progress of our time we secure the inheritance of all the treasures of the past.

Lack of personality does not constitute the traditional mind, any more than lack of initiative constitutes obedience; or lack of invention, reason.

To get away from old things passing themselves off as tradition it is necessary to go back to the farthest past—which will reveal itself to be the nearest present.

Just as "bourgeoise morality" is not the true Christian morality, and the intellectuality of a lot of so-called good thinkers is not real intelligence, so a conformist "orthology" cannot suffice for a true believer.

All the formulas, all the precautions of ortho-doxy, all the scruples of literal conformity, all barriers, in a word, are powerless to safeguard the purity of the faith. If the spirit should be lacking, dogma becomes no more than a myth and the Church no more than a party.

"To push piety to the point of superstition", said Pascal, "is to destroy it." To push orthodoxy to the point of religious purism is also to destroy it.

Credulity, sectarianism, and sloth are three natural tendencies of man. Too often he canonizes them under nobler names.

Non quia durum aliquid, ideo rectum, aut quia stupidum, ideo sanum. (SAINT AUGUSTINE, *City of God*, Book 14, Chapter 9.)

A man's faith can go down to zero without even being shaken by doubt. At the same time that it becomes empty and external, passing by degrees from life to conformism, it can become hard and take on the appearance of the most beautiful firmness; the bark has hardened: the trunk has become hollow.

Allegiance to traditional religion, when it takes precedence over more interior motives, can become for some a kind of credulity, as it becomes for others a kind of scepticism. Whence the paradoxical meeting of these two extremes. In this "holy alliance" it is plain enough which faction will maneuver the other, arousing it, suspicious, against all living and reflective faith.

Rationalists of all breeds give men stones instead of bread. Does it not happen that some theologians and some men of the Church change into stone the bread of truth which it is their mission to distribute?

Great mystics enjoy the same privilege as great classics of every order: their most particular teachings have a universal application, and when their thought seems to become abstruse and to aim at a very special case, it is still bread for all. Every spiritual life, even the humblest, profits by following them.

"Agreement at any cost is ephemeral, but Tradition is long-lived" (J. LEBRETON).

Nothing remains intact without effort. Repetition of formulas does not assure the transmission of thought. It is not safe to entrust a doctrinal treasure to the passivity of memory. Intelligence must play a part in its conservation, rediscovering it, so to speak, in the process.

So that the river of tradition may come down to us we must continually dredge its bed.

"God is Charity", says Saint John. We can reverse the proposition and say "Charity is God." Then if a man is truly charitable, that man cleaves to God. He possesses within him the three theological virtues. *Ubi dilectio proximi, ibi necessario etiam delectio Deo.* (SAINT AUGUSTINE, Sermon 83 on Saint John.)

We must believe in the substantial and divine reality of Charity, as in that of Truth, Justice and

Wisdom, as Malebranche and the Platonists believe in the substantial reality of Ideas.

Qui manet in caritate, in Deo manet.

Having charity, we have God in us. So the life of charity, the life of union with God, is no different from eternal life. Charity is a value in itself; that is to say that it will last forever. It is not something relative and incomplete; neither is it, therefore, something provisional: Saint Paul was right in opposing what is *echmerous* to what is *teleion*. Absolute, perfect, definite, eternal: it is all one.

Everything that has an absolute value is inscribed by that very fact in the absolute.

Eternal life is not a life for the future. By charity we start eternity right here below. *Manet caritas.*

We must come to see that God is not so much the cause of moral obligation or the sanction of duty as the very substance of Good. Then what we call the moral proof brings us in one leap to the true God, revealing himself as God of Charity.

If it does not suffice, in order to ground our obedience to the divine law, to show that God is our authentic and sovereign Master, it is because this obedience, in order to be complete, needs more than the submission due even such a Master.

We owe God the free gift of ourselves. We owe Him an intimate assent, a love, which is justified or even made possible only if God is Love and has loved us first.

Just as faith is a principle of understanding, so obedience must be a principle of freedom. You do not deliver yourself into the hands of authority like a man tired of using his initiative, abdicating; or like a sailor happy to find a quiet harbor at last after a stormy passage. On the contrary, you receive from authority the *Duc in altum*. You entrust yourself to it as to a ship leaving port for a glorious voyage and high adventure.

Any authority is necessarily a teacher. It is only because we are still en route and our future state is not yet unfolded *(nondum apparuit quid erimus)*

that, in the voice of God our Father, we come to discern the Master commanding us and so have a strict feeling of obligation. It is for the same reason that there is a hierarchical authority in the Church. When God will be whole in everyone, in the Church Triumphant, the City of the Elect, there will no longer be any other hierarchy than that of charity.

Authority is ultimately based on charity, and its *raison d'être* is education. The exercise of it, in the hands of those who hold any part of it whatever, should then be understood as pedagogy.[1]

Some people are afraid of such an idea, probably because they fail to understand it. To impose conditions on the exercise of authority, to justify it only as a means of pedagogy, instead of recognizing it simply as a right; to look upon it first of all

---

[1] This is the teaching of Saint Bernard, among others. He requires the submission of man to the external authority of revelation on the ground that our conscience, here below, is not yet adult: *"Obsecro vos, novellae plantationes Dei, vos qui nondum exercitatos habetis sensus ad discretionem boni et mali, nolite sequi cordis vestri judicium, nolite abundare in sensu vestro. . . ."* (*In psalmum "Qui habitat", sermo* 3.)

A thesis very different, you see, from what a Lessing's will be on the provisory pedagogical function of revelation.

as functional: does not this, they ask, slacken obedience?

Not at all. For if this does occasionally counteract certain abuses of power, it also shows, above all, that a purely external submission, a mere return of everything to *order,* is not yet true obedience, but only its prerequisite. It indicates that ideal submission extends to obedience of the judgment, until the time comes when it will freely expand into the liberty of the children of God.

An obedience which only recognizes orders—even if, to assure the perfect execution of these orders, it calls on the will and on the judgment—is utterly insufficient. Especially in the spiritual life, which does not consist in gestures. To fulfill the prescriptions of religious authority faithfully, strictly, without any omission, is good. But if you are satisfied with that, you have not begun to *obey.* You take for an end what is still only a means, for an act what is only its condition. You violate the idea of Catholicism.

In everything that touches on essential issues, objections are always easier than answers. The animal part in man always makes itself heard more immediately than the spiritual part, and it rarely lacks the subtlety and finesse to make itself appear the more intelligent of the two.

But it is precisely this facility that is suspect with me when it comes to difficult matters; this clarity in mysterious matters; these unhesitating assertions in matters calling for reflection and study . . . this way of being smart in the presence of problems before which the truly great man must at once feel perplexed.

Life, in every realm, is the triumph of the improbable—of the impossible. So much the same for living faith. It moves mountains; it breaks open vicious circles. It gets its food from poisons and proceeds by dint of obstacles. But on the other hand, when it happens to relapse, staying nevertheless perfectly sincere, when it happens to soften or harden, everything then becomes an occasion for it to recoil. When it softens, it becomes defenseless; when it hardens, it can assimilate no longer.

The conformist looks at things—even things of the spirit—from the outside. The obedient soul sees things—even things of the letter—from the inside.

The maternal bosom of the Church is vast enough to contain the greatest minds—and the most diverse. All can find in it the shelter necessary for all. Each according to his needs, as well, life-giving forces.

III

Witness

To anyone who would give testimony the words of Jesus apply directly: "Seek ye first the Kingdom of God and his justice and all these things shall be added unto you."

Think, live, be: next try to express scrupulously what you think, what you are living, what you are.

Nothing is more contrary to the idea of testimony than the idea of popularization. Nothing is more different from apostolic work than propaganda.

"When I see my best friend coming I do not say to myself 'How am I going to manage propagandizing him?'" (PÉGUY).

The profundity of a spiritual act is in direct proportion to its author's commitment in it.

As the apostle must testify by his life, the apologist must testify by his thought.

You cannot popularize religion the way you popularize a science; neither ingenious methods nor literary gifts can succeed in doing it.

Is it not too frequently true that dogma bores us, that spirituality bores us? We replace them by a little sentimental devotion and, if we are intellectual, by a few ideas in the field of religion and philosophy, which we complacently believe profound, personal, and proper. . . .

But since such a religion is no longer alive, it no longer has in itself any power of conquest. Then we exhaust ourselves to find some methods, some tricks of trade. . . . Testimony and apostolic work are replaced too quickly by proselytism and by propaganda.

Real radiance is a centripetal force. "I will draw everything to me." The essential problem of apostolic work is accordingly the problem of what the apostle is. The essential problem of apologetics is the problem of what the doctrine is—not of course what it is in itself, but in the mind of the apologist.

The saints: "They have only to exist: their existence is a calling" (BERGSON).

Life attracts, like Joy.

Nothing excellent can come from one who aims first at a public.

The "public" is not a partner in conversation. Whoever speaks to "the public" is actually speaking to no one.

In any search for a public there is artifice, a basic insincerity that vitiates the undertaking beforehand.

The apostle touches the heart of the multitude only if he speaks out of the fullness of his own heart.

He has an anxious solicitude for the masses, but what he sees in those masses is a series of concrete men, images of God, persons, whom he wishes he could, like God himself, call by name—by that secret name which they themselves often do not know, and by which they would be revealed to themselves.

You do not really get hold of men unless you first get hold of *man*.

Public and author are correlatives. Man is a correlative of man.

The category "public" is entirely objective and artifical. It is not primarily a matter of number. The "public" is no more the masses than it is the élite. The "public" is stupid like the mob, and does not, like it, have a soul. Insofar as they form a "public" men are exterior to themselves. To think of men through the category "public" is thus to prevent yourself from reaching the human. It inevitably disregards both the value and the needs of those you wish to reach. It commits you to futility: the better adapted you deem your work, the more sterile it will in fact be.

If you absolutely must get at a public, it is a bad technique to aim at any other than the most spiritual and exacting élite. In this the criterion is not knowledge of technicalities or abstract language, esoteric doctrine or subtle problems; it is a matter of spiritual quality and of purity.

There are everywhere, scattered in the world, mystics in potentiality or in a primitive state. These, before all, are the ones who must be reached. These, by definition, do not belong to any "public". *Cor ad cor loquitur.*

The contact of a believer with a nonbeliever must take the form of a dialogue. The all-powerful action of pure sanctity alone is dispensed from it, since sanctity is not bound by any law. But the dialogue will never get underway if it is not first a dialogue with myself.

Because they are not enslaved by nature, said Péguy, they fancy that they belong to grace. Because they are not of their own time, they fancy that they belong to eternity. The science of a specialist, the doctrine of a theologian, the very fire of a mystic do not suffice to bear witness far:

but the absence or the laying aside of these gifts will suffice even less.

The ideas of testimony and of vocation are twins. May each testify according to his own vocation. The theologian should give the testimony of a theologian. His testimony is not superior to others, but it is his, the one he will be held to account for, the one he must give in order to be faithful, the one that no other can give in his place.

When the theologian does not have to stay confined in his specialist's work, it is by emerging beyond it that he will give his proper testimony, not by remaining beneath it. It is not by neglecting it or by engaging in outside activities. For the theologian to cite the need of souls, or the necessity of a current language and the superiority of concrete and living words over abstractions and technicalities, in order to avoid accomplishing the intellectual task which is his function in the Church and which normally falls upon him alone, is not to give testimony: it is a betrayal.

To dispel the illusion, reread the apologue of Saint Ignatius in the meditation on the "three classes".

Teaching, even if it be very widespread and most marvellously adapted, is not, as such, testimony—though one can testify by teaching. Scientific research, even if it be highly specialized and apparently far removed from vital problems, can become testimony.

It is not possible to cheat for long: the language of faith alone engenders faith; the exercise of charity alone engenders charity.

In everything related to testimony it is the testimony that is effective, whereas the search for effectiveness is sterile.

The logic of testimony nonetheless requires subsidiary steps, where the question of efficacy of method comes in. Testimony is not realized by disregarding the results of action. The Christian, for example, who would not make an effort to be charitable in practice, contenting himself with beautiful sentiments or beautiful gestures, would never be a witness of charity. This is because he would not be effectively charitable.

Suffering is the thread from which the stuff of joy is woven. Never will the optimist know joy.

If we wait for conditions to be "favorable" before preaching the Gospel, we shall wait, every one of us, till our last day—and indeed till the Last Day. And if the impossible happened and these "favorable" conditions we dream of were achieved one day, are we entirely certain they would not, in reality, be the worst?

Conditions scarcely seemed favorable, in Palestine, to the preaching of Jesus. When it could be thought they were, it was at the cost of the gravest misunderstandings which could be cleared away only by a strenuous refusal on the part of Jesus. It will always be the same—the apostle will always have to beware of the same illusion reappearing. In his very patience and in his long waits he will have to say to himself, here and now, with the Apostle: *Vae enim mihi est, si non evangelizavero!*[1]

---

[1] "It would go hard with me indeed, if I did not preach the Gospel", 1 Corinthians ix, 16 (Knox).

IV

Adaptation

They are wondering how to *be adapted*. They should first know how to *be*.

When an adaptation is too much sought for, it can end only in the momentariness of fashion. It is always superficial—and moreover it always arrives late. Not that it is not necessary to adapt oneself, again and forever. But the essential adaptation is spontaneous, unconscious, preliminary. As for the immediate adaptation, it asks only for a last-minute effort.

The first question is not "how to present" but "how to see" and "how to think". Otherwise the presentation either is artificial and fallacious or does not rise above the process of popularization—which can only be, in this case, a vulgar process.

Setting out deliberately to popularize, to adapt, to reach the greatest number is not illegitimate or always useless. But it infallibly condemns you to mediocre, banal, insignificant, popular work. This law no more admits exception than the law of contradiction itself.

How should Christianity be presented? How should it be adapted to those I must evangelize? A legitimate and necessary worry. But if this is the first impulse, if it too readily takes precedence over the apostle's concern for his personal development and his own evangelization, it can conceal much naive pride, even when the second of our interrogations is replaced by the following more orthodox one: How should I adapt myself? The essential question must always be, What is Christianity? How can I express it to myself? How can I open all the regions of my mind to it?

And questions like these we will never be done answering. Christianity is not an object that we can hold in our hand: it is a mystery before which we are always ignorant and uninitiated.

Found in a questionnaire: "Blessed are the meek. How can this beatitude be adapted to the present time, when the violent inherit the earth?"

Would the author of this question really suppose that in the time of Christ the meek prevailed more naturally than today over the violent? Would he believe too that in those times it was naturally pleasant to cry, to be poor, nay even to suffer persecution? Would it be his opinion, in short, that we no longer have to accept the teaching of the Beatitudes in the same sense as of old and that the time has come to "adapt" the Gospel?

Life adapts the environment to itself much more than it adapts itself to the environment.

It is not a question of adapting Christianity to men, but of adapting men to Christ.

Former generations wanted to "defend" Christianity. Today we want to "adapt" it. Two excellent intentions. But in their concern to defend it, they forgot to ask themselves what it was. Today the same danger threatens us if we are too preoccupied with adaptation.

The most necessary truths, those of which a man has the deepest need, are most often also those which are least explicitly required of him, those which he believes himself most able to do without and which he would rather not be spoken to about.

❧

If it is in a certain measure justifiable to adapt oneself to man's own conception of what he is and what he thinks, it is only for the purpose of explaining man to himself by dispelling his illusions. It is in order to lead him to see the true problems, not to solve the problems he believes his own. Perhaps in this case an elaborate adaptation would run the risk of suppressing the indispensable element of shock.

Real personality is achieved only by dint of deliberate impersonality and by self-renunciation in the search for it, and an influence that is widespread in that sense impersonal is acquired only by virtue of this personality.

"To live in your time"—this does not at all mean to let yourself be towed by fashions of the day and to share the emotions of the multitude. Deep currents alone account for eddies on the surface; they alone deserve to be attacked by an action of any magnitude.

The man who does not go down to underlying causes will never get at the heart of the evil.

How horrible the picturesque style that tries to be a substitute for profundity of life!

If you attend only to the current and vulgar objection, you can perforce bring to it only a current and vulgar answer—which will not be an answer. Giving attention to only the current and vulgar indifference, without going back to its sources, leads us likewise to oppose to it only a kind of faith, arguments, and explanations that are vulgar and current and will take no deep hold.

Everyone can see plainly that unbelief and indifference, in spite of some contrary trends, are spreading almost everywhere. Do we realize that one of the causes of this fact is that each year, through a series of obscure tragedies, deep within the *khagnes*[1] of the provinces or of Paris, or in similar milieux, many of our young élite lose their faith while discovering a universe where Christianity seems to have no place? Tomorrow they will be the educators of our youth, the molders of opinion, the most popular of our writers. Then we shall attempt—tardily, awkwardly, timidly—some efforts at refutation; we shall solicit some intervention of the Holy See; we shall improvise against them an apologetic devised for popularity, as will indeed be necessary, since it is the masses who will come under their corrosive

[1] Upper grades in secondary schools, where students prepare for the *Ecole Normale Supérieure*.

influence. Meanwhile in the same high institutions of learning the same story will be starting all over again.

If you do not live, think, and suffer with the men of your time, as one of them, in vain will you pretend, when the moment comes to speak to them, to adapt your language to their ear.

"Know the moderns in order to answer their difficulties and their expectations." A touching intention. But this way of projecting the "moderns" into an objective concept, of separating oneself from them to consider them from the outside, makes this good will useless.

The one who wants to adapt himself too much risks letting himself be dragged along.

We may praise every effort of presentation—but only if it is the result of an effort of an utterly different kind. A man who is sincere hates the "seeming" of society people, which empties them of the last drops of substance they could have. At that, he does not ape Diogenes, and he knows how to receive his friends.

The apostle disdains no activity that can open for him, even remotely, an access to souls. No form of writing, no literary style, is to de disdained either. *Haec oportet facere, et illa non omittere.*

When I teach my brother it is not really I who teach him, but we are both taught by God. Truth is not a good that I possess, that I manipulate and distribute as I please. It is such that in giving it I must still receive it; in discovering it I still have to search for it; in adapting it, I must continue to adapt myself to it.

The Communist daily *L'Humanité* did an exceptional job of popular penetration in its early days, when it was the most intellectual newspaper in Paris—and precisely because of that. There were cheap tricks in it too, of course. But these, which would suffice to explain the wide circulation of the paper, do not explain at all the penetration of minds it affected. The influence of newspapers with big or little tricks goes only so far as to inflate, to turn round and about, to lull or over-excite the passions of the masses, without ever creating in their minds the slightest new value. And yet we are here on the political plane, the most "impure" of all!

If I no longer understand a particular institution or symbol, it is perhaps because that institution or that symbol has grown old. It is perhaps also because I am myself too barbarous and new.

So it takes two convergent efforts to effect a meeting.

I knew a man—a priest—who spoke in almost the same tone in his room, in a church, and in a lecture hall; who expressed himself in almost the same terms whether before little children or among philosophers; who said the same things to the infidels or our modern society, to pagans from the Far East, and to the faithful. In his discourse, which never attained eloquence, the machinery of proof was always reduced to a minimum; there was no debate; it was as free before strangers as in a group of intimate friends. His politeness—exquisite, by the way—ignored the conventional pleasantries. Never a man, in a sense, who was less "adapted". But this man was all things to all men, and of his plenitude everybody partook.

V

Spirit

It is not with a literature of popularization, even the most intelligent and best adapted, that Christian thought will ever be created, and to the same extent that Christian thought is lacking will the very work of adaptation fail of accomplishment. Yet Christian thought is to be found nowhere in an isolated state. It does not have the objective subsistence of doctrine. It can only come into being by the intellectual effort of the Christian, and the intellectual effort provided for us by our Fathers does not dispense us from an analogous effort. For thought cannot be hoarded. It is something alive and it quickly becomes rigid, scelerotic, and dies.

Do not dwell on the faults of difficult enterprises. Perhaps their main difficulty comes from the fact that they anticipate the future. It is just when a work can be popularized that its force of penetration becomes exhausted. But great enterprises, without having to modify themselves, attain popularity by themselves, because they mold the human mind in their image: *non ego mutabor in te sed tu mutaberis in me.*

Thought is of so rare an essence that wherever we discover a manifestation of it we not only relish it but are tempted to approve of it.

It is a great illusion to believe that certain problems are ulterior and can be left to specialists, their solution being presumed not to have any effect on the plane where one has decided to remain. This assumes that problems are exterior to each other, which amounts to misunderstanding the nature of the mind.

The life of the mind can only be total.

The day comes when one sees, all at once, that all those "abstract" problems which were perhaps difficult to understand are not mere schoolwork, boring for some, interesting or even exciting for others; one sees that they are urgent problems, problems that pose the reality of life, that concern it wholly, and whose solution matters extremely. From that day on, philosophic reflection takes on a different character. It ceases to be a kind of work like any other. One no longer feels one has the right to get away from it systematically outside of the hours prescribed by the schedule; no longer the right moreover—nor the inclination—to close the door of one's inner life to it. But on the other hand, one no longer has the right to treat it with the old flippancy, no longer the right—nor the wish—to build up and tear down for the fun of it; no longer the right to trust too readily one's own insights; no longer the right to start with no matter whom and no matter what basic discussions, at the risk of sowing the seeds of trouble in oneself or in others. Sincerity then appears as a virtue not only necessary but difficult. Embarked on a serious adventure, one has the duty of thinking about it prayerfully and of treating Truth with sovereign respect.

The only "gospel truth" is the words of the Gospel. The words of the encyclicals are but encyclical words: assuredly very worthy, extremely important, but another thing.

There is a life to thought, I mean a life proper to thoughts, which is more living than any sensible life. But the one who does not know what a thought is rejects all thought in the name of life, incapable as he is of discerning the difference between living thought and dead thought. Thus certain defenders of the social order pursue, without distinguishing between them, highway robbers and prophets.

To one who has seen a problem the most beautiful and true things, uttered by someone who has not seen it, are but words and yet more words.

Conversely, to one who has not seen a problem things most real and topical, most mordant and incisive, most exactly adapted to their object, most necessary, said by one who has seen, can only seem to be levities, imaginations, complications, useless subtleties, strivings for originality, abstractions without foundation.

There is no serious study without a withdrawal, a temporary refusal which may look like a desertion, an evasion. It is however not by keeping *au courant* with daily facts or by discussing the slogans of the man on the street and the latest formulations of current objections that you live in your time and prepare for action.

Only what is rooted is living. But taking root truly will often make you seem detached.

If we are sometimes inclined to ignore the deep need of our comtemporaries for religion, is it not because the men in whom these needs are incarnated most strongly are those whom we do not meet, or those whom we run into as enemies? But in this the less insight we have, the more abusive negation we draw from our short experience: men instinctively turn their backs on one who they feel is not for them a bearer of light. "One never hears any questions except those to which one can find the answer" (NIETZSCHE).

A continuity is indispensable between theological work, apostolic action, and the currents of spiritual life. This continuity does not run only one way: there must be action and reaction, exchange. Theology, apostolic action, spirituality: each of these three functions is essential and none of them can be exercised authentically without the contribution and help of the other two. A theologian who, even in his work of theologian, would be cut off from the apostle and the spiritual man within himself could not properly accomplish this work. Conversely, how many dangers to the apostle and the spiritual man, if the theologian in them happens to be lacking! How many deviations, and besides how many failures! The theologian receives and he gives in turn. He expresses and he guides.

"All things", says Pascal, "are causing and caused."

The spirit, in order to spread as well as to flourish, needs conditions which are not too favorable. Too much liberty weakens it and takes away its substance. If in fact it neither flourishes nor spreads, that must not be explained too readily by reference to the obstacles it meets. It is mainly an interior deficiency that should be diagnosed.

People dream about conditions of life which would secrete spirit naturally. That is a great illusion.

The only possible existence for the spirit is "a roving ever threatened life. . . ."[1] The most insidious threat is that hidden under favor.

Before it can be adapted in its presentation to the modern generation, Christianity in all necessity must, in its essence, be itself. And once it is itself, it is close to being adapted. For it is of its essence to be living and always of the time.

The big task consists then in rediscovering Christianity in its plenitude and in its purity. A task which is always and ceaselessly called for, just as the work of reform inside the Church itself is called for always and ceaselessly. For even though Christianity is eternal, we are never once and for all identified with its eternity. By a natural leaning we never cease losing it. Like God Himself, it is always there, present in its entirety, but it

[1] An adaptation of the closing verse of Vigny's poem *La Maison du Berger*. The words give the sense of the concluding stanza rather than the actual words of the poet.

is we who are always more or less absent from it. It escapes us in the very measure that we believe we possess it. Habit and routine have an unbelievable power to waste and destroy.

But how should we rediscover Christianity if not by going back to its sources, trying to recapture it in its periods of explosive vitality? How should we rediscover the meaning of so many doctrines and institutions which always tend toward dead abstraction and formalism in us, if not by trying to touch anew the creative thought that achieved them? How many explorations into distant history such a research supposes! How many painful reconstructions, themselves preceded by long preliminary work! In a word, how much "archeology"! The task is not for everyone, obviously, but it is indispensable that it be done and forever done again. Let us not think that it is possible to reach the goal cheaply: to try that would be a kind of fraud, and when it comes to essential goods, the crook is never successful.

It took forty years in the desert to enter into the Promised Land. It sometimes takes a lot of arid archeology to make the fountains of living water well forth anew.

The more profound a work is, the less its antecedents explain it. We must, in order to understand it, evaluate what will come of it or—if it is still too early—guess at it.

Sincerity is fidelity. Man's perfection is a must-be. He does not merely *have,* he *is* a vocation. Sincerity is fidelity to one's vocation since it is fidelity to oneself.

Outside of that, there is only a series of superficial and contradictory tendencies, psychological dilettantism, or paralysis and disintegration.

The question is not to know whether Christians are always very intelligent (we know very well they are not): it is to know whether Christianity is true.

The question is not to know whether Christians have always done what was expected or should have been expected of them (we know very well they have not): it is to know whether Christianity is necessary to the world.

❧

Everything, in the world, is the object of knowledge, actual or potential—everything, except the
spirit which builds up that knowledge (and, how
many other things there are, too, that go with
that invisible, impalpable spirit, that dimensionless point!)—everything, except that oper-
ative power forever at work and forever escaping,
a shuttle that can never be caught, as it ever moves
over to the opposite side to that where science
waits to catch it.

You might think it enjoyed letting itself be
grasped: this time, we have got it, we make it
fast, measure it, analyze it, we heave the lead into
its very depths. We make all sorts of discoveries
there. We apply methods which have been so
successful in the exploration of external nature or
of social nature—and this time too, the results are
surprising! Yes, they are fine results. But it is not
spirit you have in your hands!

The mystery of spirit is a mystery which cannot be provisional, which is always intact again
after each apparently successful attempt to lay
hold on it. It is not the mystery of the unexplored, but of the inexplorable. It is, however, a
mystery more luminous, apprehended by more
immediate and intimate knowledge, than the
most definite, the most thoroughly mastered ob-

ject of science. All the same, it is an everlasting and stimulating enigma. Through it man is for ever kept on the alert; for ever he is forced to seek, forced to wonder—with a wonder quite different from that which he feels when confronted with the riddles of nature, in quite a different quest than that which he makes outside himself. . . .

VI

Incarnation

Words end by having no meaning when they have all meanings at once. Everyone today demands the "incarnation" of Christianity in life, everyone claims membership in a Christianity "incarnate". But this unanimity covers the confusion of Babel.[1]

[1] It is of course understood that all the paradoxes in this chapter suppose, far from contesting it, the necessity of an insertion—or as they say today so expressively, an incarnation—of Christianity in the temporal order. These paradoxes attack only the counterfeits, or invite us to push on farther, not to fall short of it. In fact, we could do no better than to quote the words of Msgr. Salière on Catholic Action. They express the law of all of Christian life:

"By incarnating itself in everyday reality, Catholic Action gains in extent, in profundity, in effectiveness. . . . Catholic Action can be effective only if it is incarnated in temporal institutions, spirit in matter. Through these institutions it sets atmospheres, it directs social pressure. . . . I do not

We must avoid a certain confusion which would be fatal. Some of those who speak today of adapting Christianity would like, at bottom, to change it. Some of those who would like, they say, to "incarnate" it more would like, at bottom, to bury it. Christianity must not become "the religion of which one can make what one will" (FRANZ OVERBECK).

A wish to "incarnate" Christianity sometimes really leads to disincarnating it, emptying it of its substance. It becomes lost, buried in politics or in sociology or, at best, in morality.

A Christianity which shirks the urgent tasks of charity toward the most miserable and the most abandoned, a Christianity which refuses testi-

---

understand a refusal to act in the temporal sphere, a refusal on the part of spirit to inform matter. The union of the spiritual and the material, of the eternal and the temporal, is the situation of the human beings we are. . . . By incarnating itself, Catholic Action quits the dream and impregnates the real, the social, the material, the economic, and the temporal. It acts." (*Action catholique incarnée,* Feb. 7, 1945.)

mony by consenting to reduce to a pinpoint the precise part of the Credo which at the very moment is threatened—there you have a Christianity disincarnate. The rest is verbiage.

We surrender to instincts of the flesh and blood, overcome by disgust for the spiritual life; we fall into all the illusions of naturalism, and we call this "Christianity incarnate".

An "Aryan Christianity" is a Christianity perfectly incarnated: in it one is Christian only by carnal birth.

What a beautiful plan for Christianity incarnate Satan presented to Jesus, in the desert! Jesus preferred a Christianity crucified.

Shall we consent to make of the incarnation what, in Pauline language, is called the suffocation of the Spirit?

Beware lest the obsession to save the masses tempt us into seducing them with vulgar attractions, similar to those used by their temporal masters. Saint Peter and Saint Paul, arriving in Rome, did not try to find some substitute for the amphitheater to offer the pagan masses.

Should reference to the mystery of the Incarnate Word be a means of blaspheming the mystery of the crucified and resurrected Word? *Absit!*

The mystery of Christ is ours also. What was accomplished in the Head must be accomplished also in the members. Incarnation, death, and resurrection: that is, taking root, detachment, and transfiguration. No Christian spirituality is without this rhythm in triple time. We have to make Christianity penetrate to the deepest human realities, but not let it be lost or disfigured there. It must not be emptied of its spiritual substance. It must act in the soul and in society as a leaven raising the whole dough; it must supernaturalize all. It must put a new principle at the heart of everything; it must make the exigency and urgency of the call from above resound everywhere.

If Christ was not truly man, conceived, and born of woman, He would not truly be our Savior. But if He had not also really died and been resurrected, then our faith in Him would be vain and we would not be saved. Death and resurrection do not destroy the work of incarnation; they consummate it. They do not go back over it, effecting a disincarnation; they lead toward the goal, by spiritualizing even the flesh. Thus a spiritual Christianity, a Christianity which puts the sign of the cross on everything and which accepts no human value without taking care to transform it, is not a disincarnated Christianity; it is the only authentic Christianity, the only one in which the "incarnation" is not a snare.

Christ did not come to do the "work of incarnation" but the Word was incarnated to do the work of redemption.

Our incarnate God is a crucified God. The

Word made flesh is God dying in His flesh and being reborn in the Spirit.

We do not want a religion that is outside of life. All right. But what is life? We must take it as a whole. What life would be worth our love and our attention that would not reach eternal life? We want an "incarnate" religion and that's all right, too. We want it to be wholly, in all its proceedings, under the sign of the incarnation. Let us not be half-way logical, but follow to the end the way that the Incarnation opens to us. Let us not break the rhythm of the Christian mysteries, which call for one another and are linked together. The Word of God, in incarnating itself, sets the first act of an unbreakable series, where it is followed by death, resurrection, and finally ascension. Our religion, if it is incarnated and fully established in human life, must, to be faithful to Christ, implant there the cross, so as to introduce the life-giving death without which there is no glorious resurrection. But, as we are terribly and almost incurably carnal, the very resurrection of the Savior risked being misinterpreted by us. Accordingly, the resurrection is succeeded by the ascension, to show us what it meant and to force us finally to turn our eyes upward, to go beyond the earthly horizon and all that pertains to man in his natural state. Thus the lesson of the ascension does not contradict the lesson of the incarnation: it prolongates it, deepens it. It does not set us beneath or apart from life; it obliges us to assume it fully while aiming beyond.

Humanize before Christianizing? If the enterprise succeeds, Christianity will come too late: its place will be taken. And who thinks that Christianity has no humanizing value?

It has been and still is indispensable, in opposition to the falsely supernatural illusions of an airy apostolate, as well as the pharisaism of the privileged, to insist upon the economic and social conditions without which it would be vain to preach the practice of Christian virtues to the masses. More profoundly, it is good to react against certain social structures which, being dehumanizing, are the natural enemies of any faith. But do not go thinking that faith and Christian virtues would flourish automatically in a society where these obstacles would have been removed. A living seed fructifies in the most unpromising ground, and, without sowing, the best soil will always be barren. The question of the seed will always remain the essential question. The religious problem, everywhere and always, is essentially a problem of the spiritual order. The deepseated causes of dechristianization and the profound factors of rechristianization will always be of the spiritual order.

It is when the spiritual seed loses some of its vigor, when the religious principle does not face its responsibilities, that the Marxist theory of religion becomes true. In periods of lessened religious vitality, even if religion holds an important place on the surface, it is more true than any other theory. The spiritual life is a continuous creation: to the extent that it gives way, materialistic explanations prevail against it.

There was a time when professed materialism constituted a reaction of noble souls against an official spirituality, hypocritical or weak. Is not the time approaching when it shall be necessary, for the sake of a real fidelity to the Incarnation, to break with a word worn out from having been used too much? It will be necessary, in reaction, to speak a little more of souls. . . .

"Jesus came for the poor, you say. Yes, doubtless. But he came for the rich too, so that they might become poor out of love, and you cannot ignore the fact that hundreds of thousands of saints have obeyed: Jesus came for souls, that's what we must say" (LÉON BLOY).

As soon as one speaks of a spiritual apostolate, some will cry out "angelism". Why do they not attack Saint Paul? According to them, will it not be angelism to exalt the "spiritual man"? Will it not be disincarnating Christianity to declare "The Lord is Spirit"?

The love of souls: it is not abstract nor narrow. To love the soul in another is to love his particular vocation, to love him as God loves him, such as he is, unique.

We must rehabilitate the word *soul*. "To save one's soul": one may have sometimes harbored under this formula an egoistic worry over one's own salvation, a cowardly or puerile despising of worldly tasks. But such is not its evangelic meaning! I do not have to win the world, even for Christ: I have to save my soul. That is what I must always remember, against the temptation of success in the apostolate. And so I will guard myself against impure means. It is not our mission to make truth triumph, but to testify for it.

In the same measure that, by lack of faith, we believe our spiritual universe dependent on the economic, social, political, and even intellectual conditions of our milieu, it becomes so actually. The illusion generates itself and changes into reality. From then on, the one who is the victim of it can be proud of his realistic perspicacity. . . .

That is what constitutes for many the seduction of explanations of the Marxist type. Man is not an objective and invariable datum: he always more or less shapes himself, unconsciously, on the idea that he forges of himself; and when, within him, the spirit no longer considers itself master and first inspirer, man becomes indeed the slave or at least the follower. But then it reaches the point where it is no longer spirit. The spirit has gone some place else. In some other men, who orient themselves in another direction, it has recovered its mastery. Thus it remains first always, though perhaps in an imperceptible position. At the beginning of any new path taken by humanity there is an invention, a creation of the mind; there is a choice, a spiritual option, that can be explained by itself and by nothing else.

VII

Disinterestedness

Any culture is disinterested. All contemplation is also. But from this disinterestedness, all real influence flows. It comes as a result; it could not be a goal.

Nothing fecund is achieved, in the order of mind, by utilitarian pursuits. We must repudiate all pragmatic preoccupations if we want to obtain substantial and durable fruits.

With the restrictions of the rules of transposition which, on the one hand, discretion and modesty require and which, on the other hand, the subject treated necessitates, the ideal would be to write nothing but what one needs to bring out of oneself, under the necessity of liberating oneself from it, in some way, by bringing it to light.

Ne cures invitationem turbae legentium (SAINT AUGUSTINE): Have no concern to please the multitude of readers.

The "method of immanence" is the very contrary of a method of complacency.

"He was writing only for himself" (ETIENNE PASCAL, preface to the *Pensées*).

"He is honest, because he speaks to himself and for himself" (NIETZSCHE, about Schopenhauer).

The pursuit of adaptation brings along, like its shadow, the pursuit of success. But what will the norm of this success be? Will it be obtained when everybody will have been pleased, when everybody will have understood, and when no as-tonishment or scandal will have been provoked? Such a success greatly risks being merely the mark of ineffectiveness. Nothing strong, nothing new, nothing urgent penetrates man's mind with-out crossing resistance. Or would you think that Christian preaching should no longer be "scan-dal" and "folly" in the eyes of the world?

The very success of an extreme popularization is sometimes, in religious matters, a disaster. Mr. X, for example, a brilliant professor, attracts a large audience to his classes and thus sheds, as everyone sees and acclaims, Christian influence. But on each occasion a few young men and girls, less docile, more demanding, not daring perhaps to stand opposed to the enthusiastic atmosphere, clench their fists in silence. These will be the masters tomorrow. . . .

Remember too the concentrated anger of a Proudhon reading, in his youth, the apologists in vogue in 1830.

The *Cahiers de la Quinzaine* were not at all best-sellers. As for the first *Jeanne d' Arc,* it sold only one copy. I have known the time when it was impossible to confess a liking for Péguy without being accused of snobbery. A Pierre Lasserre was making those who appreciated Péguy devotees of a literary sect, and the stream of cultured men was taking his word for it. The best disposed were thinking that such an idealist could not exercise any real influence anyway, and that such an ultra-original author would be the least destined of any to be known by the people.

Today Péguy is a classic. He has penetrated everywhere. He is one of the most readily understood of all our authors. His great French and Christian themes find an echo everywhere. Everyone marvels that no deforming intellectualism isolates him as it does many others. The working class are already reading him. He is shut only to the Philistines. I am afraid that looking too soon for a large audience will bring, at best, only an audience of these Philistines.

We don't have to guess what the future will be, but to see what the present necessitates. We don't have to calculate our chances, but to consider our duty.

"You are mistaken, my friend, when you say that a man who is good for anything ought to calculate his chances of living and dying. Nay, the only thing he must consider when he acts is whether what he does is right or wrong, and whether he acts like a good man or a bad one" (Socrates, PLATO, *Apology*).

"You are helping that kind of poor people?" says this well-meaning Catholic to me. "Watch out. Those people won't be grateful to you at all and tomorrow you'll find them against you." I will admit that this might not be calumny. But what does it matter? Does not my religion give me the duty of helping them? That is the only consideration. A Christian does not help his neighbor to profit by it. *Nonne ethnici haec faciunt?* should we reduce the Gospel to a clannish morality?

Borrowing from politics the idea of *success* by propaganda; borrowing from economics the idea of *yield* by rationalization: would this be all that the incarnation of the apostolic work, of its methods and of its ends, amounts to?

If you are not exacting about the end, there is still less reason for being so about the means. The less human the end, the more the means—according to increasing proportion—can afford to be inhuman without inconvenience: because means and end are then more and more heterogeneous.

All *human* effectiveness supposes at least a certain amount of disinterested activity. Now any other kind of effectiveness is not worth seeking. Moreover, it would be harmful, being dehumanizing.

Does success consist in "arriving"? Or does it consist in realizing the grand program which motivated the legitimate desire for arriving?

Christianity is never triumphant.

It is not the proper duty of Christianity to form leaders—that is, builders of the temporal—although a legion of Christian leaders is infinitely desirable. Christianity must generate saints—that is, witnesses to the eternal.

The efficacy of the saint is not that of the leader. The saint does not have to bring about great temporal achievements; he is one who succeeds in giving us at least a glimpse of eternity, despite the thick opacity of time.

Effectiveness, even when temporal, must be the sign—always limited, precarious, difficult to interpret—of authentic Christianity. But a Christianity which would seek temporal efficacy first would not be authentic and it would not even attain the looked-for result.

If it can be said that a first rough draft of Christendom was effected in the Middle Ages it is because believers then were looking towards the eternal.

Despising man is foresighted and effective whenever it is a matter of using the mechanism man for some egoistic and precise end. But this is blind and ineffectual if it is on the contrary a matter—and the thing is not impossible—of awakening, of exalting, of transforming.

It is because a certain N. thought for himself, searched for himself, made an effort to express to himself, with all possible rigor and sincerity, what he was thinking, what he was believing, that he has obtained, without having aimed at it, so large an audience. He put himself into his work with all his Christian faith, all his mystic soul, all the culture of his learning, all his needs as an unsatisfied intellectual. He lived; he has reached the living. More than that, he created some life. He made some minds that were hesitating at the crossroads follow his path. And it is because he thus first won over a handful of his contemporaries whose minds had a secret harmony with his own that afterwards—and very rapidly—his voice echoed deep down in the masses. He found what he had not been searching for. Which does not mean that apostolic ardor did not have much to do with the source of his endeavors in thought. A Christian who searches is, in his innermost efforts, searching with everyone for everything.

VIII

Socialization

"Seek ye first the Kingdom of God." Whereas the Christian social order is an ideal looked for in the future, the Kingdom of God is already here, mysteriously present. For eternity, which is beyond the future, is not exterior to the present like the future. The Christian social order still belongs to the realm of objective things, of exterior things which occur in time; it is part of the shape of the passing world: the Kingdom of God is the spiritual reality, interior and eternal. We try to realize the first by progressing in time, but we enter the second by a passage which is always more or less a rupture as well as a consummation: a passage from time to eternity.

To live in the eternal and to contemplate things, as far as it is possible for us, from the point of view of eternity, is not at all to put ourselves, as they say, in an ivory tower. It is not to refuse to take part in anything nor to raise ourselves in a pretentious way above the mêlée. It is on the contrary to place ourselves at the heart of the most real reality, just as God is at the heart of everything, and to model our judgment as far as possible on the very judgment of God. It is then to become committed, when necessary, much more deeply than if we remained at the point of view of time, which is always relative.

A state of social perfection would not be a state of things where the social order would be realized to perfection. It would be a state of things where there would no longer be any need for what we call the social order. That is to say that this concept is totally eschatological.

A most perfect social order can be a world of dead souls. It even has more of a chance of being such than any other.

The social order is not only a flowering out into
society of Christianity lived within souls. It is also
a safeguard against that paganism which always
persists inside of us. It is not the sign of the
triumph of the new man, but it is rather one of
the necessary aspects of the eternal war against the
old man.

We must constantly take care that an activity that
does not disregard the social consequences of the
Gospel remains faithful to the evangelical inspiration, lest it turn into a dream of eudaemonism or
into a kind of social humanism which would be
largely chimerical and which would tend to identify the "Christian social order" with the Kingdom of God.

Belief in sin prevents us from Utopia, but it
should not deter us from seeking for social progress. On the contrary, it encourages us to it by
showing us its necessity. If man were naturally
good, we would only have to let things take their
course. But against his unruly tendencies and his

weaknesses we have to build a whole network of dikes, by means of as perfect a social organization as possible. This is indeed a very insufficient work, doomed to failure, if it is not accompanied by an effort at education. A real social order cannot remain purely external. Yet the task has to be undertaken. Those who refuse to do it in the name of the dogma of sin are no more within the logic of Christian dogma than they are in accord with the Church.

Institutional Christianity seems to everyone like the most conservative and opportunist force there is; whereas Christian thinking, when exercised in its purity, shows itself on the contrary as the most revolutionary, most unsatisfied power, and the most loaded with the absolute.

Here we have, at first sight, a paradoxical contrast. Now this contrast is not only due—as a superficial interpretation could explain it—to the fact that the first (institutional Christianity) has in its charge weighty concerns and at the same time feels a natural affinity with all established power and has an innate taste for order (even understanding all this in the noblest sense), whereas the second (Christian thinking) judges the world with sovereign liberty and rejects any compromise with the injustice and lying which always reign in this world. The true explanation is very different, and really there is no contrast. Christian organization and thinking express, each in its own way and according to a legitimate and necessary division of labor, one fundamental attitude. It is for the same and unique reason that unique Christianity, in its double aspect—institutional and doctrinal, social and reflective—is, on the one hand, most conservative and, on the other, most revolutionary. It is both, in a supreme way. It is both simultaneously, and this double character is but the expression of its unique essence.

Christianity knows that it is not of this world, that any formula of this world is more or less evil, and that it must, nonetheless, accommodate itself to all of them without ever ceasing to testify against evil.

Whence these conflicts, tragic from the outset, which occur not only nor even mainly between the upholders of authority or the social cadres on one side and those who bear in mind the demands of Christian thinking on the other; but, more intimately, within the same Christian conscience, there are these conflicts between detachment and attachment, between submission and condemnation, acceptance and refusal. Beyond the different attitudes that obviously govern the difference in régimes, governments, and temporal acts, the same basic attitude remains, apparently contradictory, the source of ever-renewed heart-breaks.

A facile solution—the only one, in truth, which can be imagined—would be the escape upwards, the mystical escape. But if, in a sense, some persons do escape—and it would not be justifiable, putting it mildly, to set them up as models for everyone—the Church for its part cannot manage to escape. Placed by its founder in the midst of the world, it must there accomplish its task, which is not of this world. Consequently there it remains, always militant, always tormented within. Always loyal yet always estranged. Always here yet always looking elsewhere. There will always be observed in it, together, that kind of conspiracy *with* the established power, which shows itself openly, challenges public opinion and often scandalizes it, and that other kind of conspiracy *against all* established power, which never ceases to disquiet the most clear-sighted statesmen. Even if we suppose that the Church will always be (what is not humanly possible) perfectly free and perfectly wise in its leaders as well as its prophets, it will not avoid seeming either enslaved or belligerent to those who have not penentrated its inner essence.

The Church will always discourage revolutionaries dreaming of having her for an ally; she will always draw from them the reproach of detachment, of lack of a deep interest in their cause, even when her goal and theirs seem to coincide in some things. But she will not inspire more confidence in the conservatives or in the holders of authority, who will always feel that she escapes them in the depths of herself, even when she appears to be one of their supporters; they will always have the feeling that she refuses to consider their order absolute and that she incessantly introduces in it a principle of dissatisfaction.

All men *of this world,* especially the best of them, if they are only of this world, will be scandalized by the Church. Whether conservative or progressive they will always get impatient with finding her reticent and lukewarm—though she is, at bottom, more committed and more ardent than they think. From either group she is in fact detached. She is the Church *of God.* The witness of divine things among men, she already inhabits eternity.

How much simpler it would be to suppress forever all these insoluble conflicts between Church and State! Why should not one of the two powers absorb the other? Why not a Church tailored to the citizen or a State taking care of the whole man?

Yes, it would be much simpler. But if the nature of man is twofold, could any simple solution be anything but an error? Tyranny too is simpler than liberty. It suppresses all its inconveniences, as the doctor who kills his patient relieves him of all his suffering. And what would man be and what would society be, if all conflict found in them would have been banished?

A social paradise can be a spiritual hell; in which case, however, it would stop very quickly being even a social paradise. It can also be simply a spiritual desert, and if it lasts then, it can only be at the price of a diminished, atrophied humanity. This is why, just as it would be a hypocrisy to neglect social work as long as the never-ending work of spiritual education is not completed, all the same it would be inhuman to let man ignore his highest nobility, to divert him from himself and to stifle in him his nostalgia for his divine country, as long as the indispensable social work is not achieved—which doubtless is forever un-achievable. We have to apply here, just reversing it, the Marxist directive according to which revolutionary activity and the fight against religion must go along shoulder to shoulder, for total liberation. Both efforts, social and spiritual, must proceed simultaneously and can proceed only that way. Each is a guarantee of the seriousness and authenticity of the other. Without concern for its social and temporal consequences, the spiritual life is distorted; without a deepening of spirituality all social progress remains unworthy of man and can finally turn against him. God, for whom man is made, can only be reached by their convergence.

Belief in eternity does not tear us away from the present, as we are sometimes told, to make us lost in dreams: it works just the other way. It is rather by disregarding eternity that Christians have disregarded their times. And those who have only an earthly future in view run no less a risk of being separated from their times, though in another manner. For this future as such is entirely exterior to the present. Consequently they risk becoming inhuman toward their contemporaries; in wishing to serve a humanity which eludes them, they risk neglecting, despising, using, sacrificing their brothers, all these men of flesh and blood, these men with the potentiality for infinity and the need for eternity which are in them. And if it was a question only of sacrificing their physical life and so to speak the animal part of their being!

As fashionable as the word "commitment" is, the actual thing is rare. Even sincere faith and regular practice, even real piety are still far from a fully committed Christianity.

Commitment presupposes a profound and ardent faith which does not stop at a faith of pure obedience but which inspires enthusiasm from within and must be a source of resolute activity. It presupposes a persevering tendency to reduce the gap which always subsists between theory and practice. It is not satisfied by that verbal inflation which is perhaps one of our worst faults. Ancient Roman liturgy can here teach us a lesson, by the steady and reserved sobriety of its prayers. Christian faith and sentiments require sober expression: but it must be felt that we are ready to act according to them, ready to give testimony.

Moreover, let us not confuse Christian commitment with a temporal commitment. The latter can be a duty; it can, in certain cases, impose itself urgently on a Christian, but it is something else.

Christian profession is, before all, a requirement of *spiritual* commitment. A requirement of commitment to the celestial city, the first city to a Christian. *Non habemus hic civitatem permanentem. Nostra conversatio in caelis est.*

Before being a hope for the future, eternal life is a requirement for the present.

The more a priest is conscious of his high spiritual mission and is really faithful to it, the more he has the right—because he has the corresponding duty—of detaching himself from purely political problems and human concerns. His attitude toward established power will then appear to be made up of both conciliatory loyalty and a certain indifference, to the extent that some will think him too servile and others too remote. They will accuse him also of accepting changes in régime too easily and quickly, and of conforming to the changing political orthodoxies. Provided he remains independent the priest must accept being so badly understood, not only by adversaries but even by men of good will, by sincere men who are sometimes close to him. His attitude will be neither denial nor desertion of the human cause— and this will be apparent when the occasion arises. It will be active and rational fidelity to his character of "man of God". Given wholly to his Father's business, the priest, in the image of Christ, whose messenger he is, introduces his brothers to a share in it.

IX

Truth

Theology has been greatly reproached for reducing all thought to slavery.

To which it may be replied in the first place that, at least, the situation it established was clear. The believer, indeed, unequivocally declares that he submits his intelligence to Faith. How much so-called free thought is hypocritically enslaved!

It is fitting to observe in the second place that theology has not failed to set its slave free. Its confidence in the strength and unity of the true, like its esteem for the value of the spirit, was great enough for that. Theology itself declared of philosophy: *non ancilla nisi libera.*[1] And though there have been individual illusions about this, that declaration was not intended to remain platonic.

[1] "She is no handmaid if not free."

Today, we see many "doctrines" constructed out of figments, in the service of ends which either interest or passion dictates. And thought is often seen to be reduced to slavery by command of an atheistic doctrine which in the first place was willed. Beforehand, with no reference to thought, all the stakes are laid. Thought is compelled to make the ratification.

Our ideas grow old with us, that is why we pay no particular attention to them, and we are quite astonished at younger minds not falling in love with them in their turn, as we did.

When we cease to understand a thing, we make fun of it. Perhaps, indeed, that thing no longer deserves to be understood; perhaps, on the other hand, making fun is entirely silly. In the one case as in the other—whether the fault lies with the thing or the scoffer—if there is no refutation, often there is at least—and perhaps sometimes it is something more in actual fact—the judgment of history.

But history, too, will be judged.

Ideas wear out quickly. Words rot more quickly still. And when thought itself is tainted, it proportionately corrupts all the words to which recourse is had in the hope of putting it right again.

Our age offers us more than one glaring example, especially with these three big words: community, incarnation, transcendence. Restored to honor to call us to the "One Thing Necessary", the old word transcendence is at once adopted and diverted by a thought that time makes enchanting, in order to set that One Thing Necessary aside.

Changes which count are never gratuitous. They derive from the putting of new questions, demanding original answers. The cult of up-to-dateness has never had anything to do with it.

So all thought necessarily has its situation. And as, in a more or less brief space of time, each new answer begets new problems, thought is always on the move. Consequently, all intelligence is of necessity open. If it closes on itself, whatever wealth it has garnered, it cannot keep its treasure intact. It dries up, evaporates, or goes rotten.

That is what you see even in cases where thought partakes most of what is eternal. The believer who claims to abide once for all by such and such a stage in the expression of faith—whether his preference retains him in the fifth, the twelfth, or the nineteenth century—that man, ceasing to believe and think with the living Church, not only forgoes new gradations or new degrees of precision, he loses reality, the very substance of faith.

Ideas follow tanks—with alarming readiness and rapidity. But they were not born of the tanks. And when under the protection of the tanks, they settle on all the squares and pour down from all the platforms, then it is that in the darkness of a stable which unknowingly thwarts all the wiles of the tank-owners, is born the new idea, to whom victory is promised.

From the truest truth to the falsest falsehood, there is often only one step. It has often been noted, quite rightly. But from the noting of that fact to the condemning of certain truths, as being dangerously near falsehood, there is also one step, and that step as well is often taken, this time very wrongly.

The fear of falling a prey to error must never prevent us from getting to the full truth. To overstep the limit, to go beyond, would be to err through excessive daring; but there are also errors of timidity which consist precisely in stopping short, never daring to go any farther than half-truths.

Love of truth never goes without daring. And that is one of the reasons why truth is not loved.

. . . We always push on farther, that is very true. We draw new inferences, make new and more subtle distinctions, "get closer to the problem". We make additions, improvements, achieve greater nicety, a higher degree of perfection. . . . By what miracle does it happen that in reality no progress is made? How is it that on the contrary we stick in the mud?—Because there is no real progress without some bringing up of matters afresh or some change of perspective, some break or some turning back, a resumption of contact with the ground of the original data. . . . Progress of the spirit does not consist in prolonging but in renewing.

Every real thinker has something naïve about him. All powerful thought has something simple and new about it. Something is passed on, but something as well begins anew with it.

Everybody has his filter, which he takes about with him, through which, from the indefinite mass of facts, he gathers in those suited to confirm his prejudices. And the same fact again, passing through different filters, is revealed in different aspects, so as to confirm the most diverse opinions. It has always been so, it always will be so in this world.

Rare, very rare are those who check their filter.

When interest is its accomplice, the spirit is never at a loss to make anything tally with anything else.

Modern "dialectics" provides it with a further opportunity in this game, by allowing it to occupy the most contradictory positions without constraint—in turn and almost simultaneously.

Seeing what his "dialectics" has become in the twentieth century, must be, I imagine, Hegel's Purgatory.

There are some who say: "We reject every partisan attitude and profess objectivity. That is the only decent attitude."

There are others who say: "We reject all dilettantism and we profess commitment. That attitude alone is worthy of man."

. . . And too often the former can believe in nothing and have not the courage to make any evaluation; they are condemned to perpetual neutrality and understand nothing thoroughly, because they are ncapable of making a choice and of self-giving.

Whilst the latter, even in their eager generosity and perhaps in the soundness of their choice, are forever making themselves unjust and sectarian by yielding to their passion. . . .

We must shun *both* dilettantism and the partisan spirit. We must both become thoroughly committed, and remain clear-headed, in the service of what is just and true. Complete success is very rare, but whoever tends in that direction, even from afar, already deserves praise.

Intelligence does not naturally look for what is "intelligent": it looks for what is true. The man who turns his intelligence away from its end by seeking intelligent things is really no longer intelligent. Brilliant as he may seem, the play of his intelligence is distorted: which is an even graver thing than if his intelligence were merely deficient. In him intelligence is dandified: it is no longer robust or healthy; it is losing its fertility.

Is intelligence a faculty of truth, or is it a faculty for the satisfaction at whatever cost of the taste for clarity, order, systematization? Is it a power of penetration into the heart of reality, or a tool for constructing architecture of the mind? Is it a means of finding something other than itself, or must it simply secrete, as it were, the forms in which it will delight?

There is a cult of intelligence which, in point of fact, betrays and mocks it, because it is not the cult of truth.

The firmness of a robust body is better than the sham stiffness of a corset. The litheness of the living is more solid than the rigidness of the corpse.

The most unbending thoughts are the most vul-
nerable to change.

We admire those minds who have a reply to everything in advance, whose thought has gone
forward beyond everything, leaving no more
room for invention than for objection on the part
of minds to come. Nothing surprises them or
bothers them, but nothing urges them, either,
towards the finer shades or towards progress.
Never do they take even a furtive look, through a
door at least ajar, towards a yet unexplored domain. The whole world seems clear to them.
Everything in them is final. The system they have
forged for themselves—or which they have
learned by heart—has no pigeon-holes missing. It
makes a contented thought for them, already
wholly established in eternity. Yet, are they quite
certain that that eternity is authentic?

Great minds, real believers, are better ac-
quainted with their ignorance. . . . *Quemad-
modum possim omnibus quaestionibus quae . . . moveri
assolent satisfacere, non invenio.*

. . . *Ipsa divina eloquia palpantur potius quam trac-
tantur a nobis, dum in multo pluribus quaerimus potius*

quid sentiendum sit, quam definitum aliquid fixumque sentimus. Et ea cautio cum sollicitudinis plena sit, multa melior est tamen, quam temeritas affirmandi[2] (ST. AUGUSTINE).

Happy are those who think they "hold", as Bossuet said, "the thread of all the business of the universe"! (*Discourse on Universal History*, Preface).

He who wants to have solutions for everything, must give up reflection, so as to have them ready made. But in that case they will not really be solutions for anything.

One hardly ever encounters closed systems of thought, except in epigons, or adversaries. Such

[2]". . . I do not know how I can satisfy all the enquiries that . . . are commonly made.

". . . In understanding the divine words themselves, surely our approach is tentative rather than assured, for in the vast majority of passages we are seeking the meaning, rather than seeing in them a clearly defined meaning. And caution in this is admittedly very troublesome, but far preferable to rash assertion."

systems are seldom the fruit of a deep fidelity or a clairvoyant animosity.

The denser the ignorance, the more enlightened it thinks itself to be.

Those who have no other concern than to "move with their times", adopting its tastes, ideas, passions, crazes, prejudices, fads—will soon be out-of-date, left behind. They are, as the saying goes, "up-to-the-minute", but a minute is soon past.

It is no good wanting to go back to a pre-critical stage. But we must get at the root of criticism, and, moreover, establish a critique of criticism.

In the face of documents taking us back to the origins of our Faith, two attitudes confront one another, equally indispensable.

The critic must always be afraid of *overcharging* the texts, of "making them say more than they do", of letting himself be affected unintentionally by all that has been subsequently got out of them. The religious man, on the other hand, dreads not understanding them in their fulness. The former must shun what is arbitrary; the latter does not want to stay on the surface. How many ingenious interpretations there are, but into which later ideas or feelings have been projected! But by way of compensation, how many literally accurate interpretations there are, commonplace and deadening! To perceive the deep truth and the fruitfulness of an experience or a thought, it is not beside the point to have explored the Tradition that has issued from it. And all the criticism in the world, even if allied with the greatest power of historical evocation, will not explain Abraham's faith, or the struggles of Elijah the Prophet, or the range of prophecy of a Jeremiah. . . . It will not let us into the intelligence of the Sermon on the Mount, or the trembling of Jesus in the Spirit.

There is the hackneyedly moralizing interpretation of those who have not studied the subject historically; and there is the narrowly historical interpretation of those who have not gone deeply into it spiritually. It is very rare that a big subject is not given over to one or the other of those two kinds of interpretation; to one or the other of those alternating forms of mediocrity.

When we are faced with a very great text, a very profound one, never can we maintain that the interpretation we give of it—even if it is very accurate, the most accurate, if need be, the only accurate one—coincides exactly with its author's thought.

The fact is, the text and the interpretation are not of the same order; they do not develop at the same level, and therefore they cannot overlay one another. The former expresses spontaneous, synthetic, "prospective", in some fashion, creative knowledge. The latter, which is a commentary, is of the reflective and analytical order.

In a sense, the commentary, if it is at all penetrating, always goes *farther* than the text, since it makes what it finds there explicit; and if it does not in fact go farther, it is of no use, since no light would then be shed by it on the text. But in another and more important sense, the text, by its concrete richness, always overflows the commentary, and never does the commentary dispense us from going back to the text. There is virtually infinity in it.

As the life of the spirit develops, it inevitably comes up against new data, giving rise to new problems. New thresholds appear, which must be crossed, without our knowing into what new domains we shall be forced to enter. Drawing back or stopping even is impossible. That would not be showing humility, but giving up; not firmness, but bewilderment; not security, but suicide. So all spiritual life, that of the intelligence like that of the soul, calls for a share of adventure. All tradition requires the finding of new things. For the intelligence as well as for the soul, fidelity is of necessity creative.

Progress or not, in the life of the spirit, as in all life, there is an irreversible quality.

We can and often we must criticize new contributions, new criticisms and new objections; but we cannot fail to take account of them. Even after complete "refutation", never is everything restored to its former balance.

We cannot "cheat centuries", or even decades.

God preserve us from ever confusing the purring of our mental habits with his Truth!

Everything is always older than we think. But he who refuses everything that seems new could not quote that maxim as his authority. On the contrary, it condemns him. He is not clinging to the old, but possibly, quite simply, to what is antiquated; to what, among the old, no longer has the strength to last or rise again in fresh forms. To what is dead—and perhaps to what was never living.

Timid minds: as soon as you begin taking seriously the fundamental ideas they are always affirming, as soon as you show a little vigor in putting into practice the things they teach, they get into a panic. It seems that no idea finds favor in their sight, unless its vitality is toned down, unless its fire has gone out. They only feel comfortable with parrot-cries. They like ideas, but in an inoffensive condition, "unprimed", that is to say, in the state of dead formulas.

Timid minds: as soon as you begin taking seriously the fundamental ideas they are always af-

We can take it for sure beforehand: he who will best answer the needs of his time will be some one who will not have first sought to answer them. It is what is found in the depths of ourselves, for ourselves, which has the chance of becoming the topical remedy and the essential sustenance for others.

All serious thought is modest. It has no hesitation in going to school and staying there a long time. It is by dint of impersonality that it makes a conquest of itself and, without seeking to do so, becomes personal.

The joy of meeting young people who are open to the life of the spirit; taking it neither for a luxury nor a delicacy; demanding that one be demanding of them; wanting to excel and knowing they will not succeed without being hard on themselves; dissatisfied with their first successes; not expecting to be flattered or to have their lives made soft for them.

But such beings are rare!

"It is said: Love in God, for the love of God, and that seems cold, conventional. That is because we do not know what it is. There is nothing more profound"[3] (DOM PIERRE BASSET).

"The true can at times appear to be improbable." But even when, by way of exception, it appears to be probable, the false is still usually preferred to it, even when it is improbable. Let's not imagine that, even in the simplest questions or in the most easily demonstrable facts, the true imposes itself easily. That is not what man is given to. Not only his inclination to evil, but a whole array of hidden forces in him make him to be the ally of what is false.

Sincerity is like happiness and perhaps like beauty: we only find it by not looking for it.

[3] Formerly Abbot of the Benedictine Abbey of Saint-Martin at Ligugé, he was, it seems, much loved. He died in 1955 and some of his sayings during his last illness have been published in the *Lettres de Ligué*.

We are only sincere when we are not thinking about it.

The man who seeks sincerity, instead of seeking truth in self-forgetfulness, is like the man who seeks to be detached instead of laying himself open to love: he can only embark on infinite and sterile complications, and the whole problem is posed afresh for him at each stage—or at each circuit of the cage. . . .

"The corruption of the best is the worst of all." But in human affairs, the best always becomes corrupted: that is the worst of all.

It is a fine thing to seek the reign of truth. It is dreadful to declare that it has come. The "reign of truth" becomes fatally identified with the reign of hypocrisy. The proportions of the one to the other vary, just as the size of a shadow varies in relation to the body. But, as the shadow inevitably follows the body, so does hypocrisy follow truth—and that shadow which is hypocrisy ever tends to grow, to deepen, till it absorbs that of which it is the shadow. When the reign of truth has at last been solidly established, then there is only the reign of hypocrisy left.

"Since the reign of truth has begun . . .": that phrase is Talleyrand's, in 1792.

In order for the spirit to develop, the conditions shouldn't be too favorable. Too much freedom softens the spirit, robs it of its earnestness. If it does not develop we ought not to ascribe this prematurely to the obstacles it encounters. We ought rather to search for some interior malfunction.

We dream of circumstances in life that would naturally "secrete" spirit. A colossal mistake.

For the spirit the only adequate existence is "a perpetually uncertain and threatened life. . . ." Its worst threat is the one hiding behind a favorable situation.

The fine careers of certain "intellectuals" are the fine lives of domestic animals. The society they serve has always coddled them. Their chief job has been to hold up a mirror to it.

It is easy to believe, without giving it too much thought, that truth consists only of the correct statement of certain relationships; that it is wholly acquired by questions and answers; that the possession of it is only the possession of the sum of accurate items of information; that it can be wholly and entirely possessed, seeing that intelligence is made for it. In short, *that it has no depth*. It is believed that it is only opposed to error, and it is not seen that it is also opposed to "futility". The thesis placed on the threshold of traditional philosophy which is so clear seems to be forgotten: *ens et verum convertuntur*.[4] For this corollary at once follows from it, that the possession of the true can be perfect only in the possession of being. Now, being infinitely overflows the capacity of our minds, in their earthly state; it is attained by them, but not truly possessed. Truth, vast and deep as being, must then also overflow our intelligence—so that it may not cease to be nourished by it. But what trouble such a simple line of argument has in bearing its fruit!

Fides meretur veritatem[5] (ABBOT WILLIAM OF ST. THIERRY).

---

[4] "Being and truth are convertible terms."

[5] "Faith is deserving of the truth." William of St. Thierry

Gaudium de veritate, gaudium de Te, qui Veritas es![6] (ST. AUGUSTINE).

⚜

"Ideas grow invisibly, with no apparent revolution; and often, after thinking we have resisted some one, we think in the end like him, as if it were of our own selves"[7] (MAURICE BLONDEL).

(1085–?1148) was a theologian and mystic, some of whose writings have been translated into English, e.g., *The Golden Epistle* (Sheed and Ward, 1930), and *Meditations* (Mowbray, 1954).

[6] "Joy in truth, joy in thee, who art Truth."

[7] Maurice Blondel (1861–1949) wrote his major works after retiring from University teaching in 1927. These are *La Pensée* (1934), *L'Etre et les êtres* (1935), *L'Action* (1936–7), *La Philosophie et l'Esprit chrétien* (1944–6), *Exigences philosophiques du christianisme* (1950). From an apologetical and theological standpoint, the main issues of his philosophy concern the role of action in religious belief, the sovereign importance of the subjective factor in the solution of the religious problem, and the transcendence and the immanence of the supernatural, which is *in* us without being *of* us. See, for a full discussion of his philosophy, *Catholicisme,* vol. ii. (Letouzey, 1950).

. . . The way of Truth is solitary, Those who set out on it are lonely . . . (ABD AL WAHID-IBN ZAID).

For our contemporaries, the most disconcerting paradox is: "Let your word be: Yes." *Est, est; non, non.*[8]

Today there would be no call for the astonishment St Paul expressed when he wrote to the Galatians: "Have I become your enemy, through telling you the truth?"

---

[8] "Yes for Yes, and No for No", Matthew v, 37 (Knox).

X

Man

We do not know what man is, or rather, we forget. The farther we go in studying him, the greater our loss of knowledge of him. We study him like an animal or like a machine. We see in him merely an object, odder than all the others. We are bewitched by physiology, psychology, sociology, and all their appendages.

Are we wrong, then, to pursue these branches of learning? Certainly not. Are the results bogus, then, or negligible? No. The fault lies not with them, but with ourselves, who know neither how to assign them their place nor how to judge them. We believe, without thinking, that the "scientific" study of man can, at least by right, be universal and exhaustive. So it has the same deceptive—and deadly—result as the mania of introspection or the search for a static sincerity. The farther it goes, the more fearful it becomes. It eats into man, disintegrates and destroys him.

The insight of criticism in the manner of Nietzsche or Freud is not being questioned. But for hundreds of years this has been going on inside the Church—only, within the spiritual world, not against it. Christians do not go in for wholesale confusion. It is the discernment of the spirit that we exercise.

Or rather, our ancestors, those spiritual masters we frequent too little, whose lessons we have unlearned too thoroughly, knew how to do that. The keen knowledge of our times would only be of use and benefit to us, if we brought it to the service of a better reading of those old spiritual masters.

The old spiritual writers were as clever in tracking down illusions as modern psychologists. No doubt, even, rather more so. But they did it by another way, which led to another end. They did it in the very name of that spirituality which many recent psychologists begin by denying, as being the global illusion. They used to purify the spring which their successors dry up.

Where are the blind? Where are the clear-sighted?

Psychologists are exploring the unconscious mind, and that is a fine thing, and no doubt they will always have a job to do, no doubt they will go on indefinitely making fresh discoveries. But it is a more urgent matter—it always will be—to transform the unconscious mind. For which purpose all the psychologists' recipes are unavailing—or, at least, inadequate. And it is not even sure that such exploration may not militate against transformation.

There are no doubt more victims of the abuse of psycho-analysis than there are cures effected by it.

The first mischief it does is to persuade people that they only need to be cured, when in fact they may need to be converted.

Moralism is the cause of much mental turmoil. But how much worse is the disintegration of morality in the judgment even of the subject himself!

Practiced without discrimination, psychology, especially the kind that is called depth psychology, expresses the belief that what it does is to track down illusions; and this diagnosis is fully confirmed, because from the very start it falsifies realities. And it is the same today for all sciences concerned with man, when they are applied to what lies beyond them, to what can in no case be their object, because it is not in fact an object.

Must we as a consequence proclaim a new bankruptcy of science? Or must we nourish a good conscience which considers itself secure from the illusions denounced by psychology? In no wise. We need only to know what we are doing, to respect the limits of each sphere of activity and, as Pascal said, not to confuse the "orders".

Psychology alone is not suited, at least in the most subtle cases, to discern the difference between the authentic and the sham, between spiritual reality and illusion. It overpowers them both and triumphs superbly over one and the other. It confuses the intoxication of wine or drugs with the intoxication of the Holy Spirit.

Patience is the elder sister of efficiency.

You cannot put man in parentheses, even for excellent objectives. Nothing is more dangerous, or rather nothing is more fatal on any assumption: for either man runs the risk of perishing thereby, through suffocation; or else, if he escapes, it is at the expense of those excellent objectives, which are compromised by this offence. And social progress is all the longer delayed.

The sociology of religion may be profitable when it is put in its proper place, and this on two counts. First, it must keep from laying claim on the whole gamut of religious science and remain at its own level. And second, it must justify the very ground of its existence by truly being *religious* sociology instead of conceiving of itself as a branch of profane sociology which equally regards both religion and irreligion as deriving from neutral presuppositions.

Both these dangers are today acute, and the second of them often wants to implant itself already at the very point of departure of a sociological research program. It would be lamentable if sociology became an alibi for an era

of religious indifference or short-sighted prag-
matism, if it sought to be a substitute for philo-
sophical research and meditation on the Gospel, if
it were to transform itself in the hands of the
faithful into an instrument for the profanation and
finally the destruction of the faith.

We speak too offhandedly of atheism as being
determined by the conditions of working life in
the modern world. We forget that atheism was
initially devised, developed and lauded by intellectuals who in no sense shared in a life of work,
and that even now atheism must continually be
inculcated from the outside upon the working
masses. If we really want to critique "abstract"
speculation in an adequate way in the name of a
realistic sociology, then, whether we like it or
not, we shall have to return to discussing truth
itself—that is, after having distanced ourselves
from sociology's easy comodities.

Self-consciousness, it is said, awakens in sin. At least
it may be said with more complete certainty that
it knows itself, from the start, as consciousness of
sin.

Auspicious knowledge, fortunate shame! God does not merely draw certain benefits from certain ills, but, through a more wonderful power than that which is behind the first creation, through the power of his creative holiness, derives *Good* from *Evil* and thereby raises us up. Truly, this is the most paradoxical example of the idea which enchanted Pascal, that our wretchedness is always at the source of our greatness. Fertile affliction, the mystery of that first moment of consciousness! *Felix culpa!* Cannot the lure of divine love yet entice us? Do we run the risk—because we ourselves are bad—of seeing in it only a tyrannical injunction, and so of rebelling? Here consciousness of sin at once intervenes, forcing us to bow our heads. And the first step is made in the way of acceptance, which will be that of deliverance. *Jam illuminari coepisti, quia inest confessio*[1] (ST. AUGUSTINE).

All the explanations of psycho-analysis, even the most accurate, and all the diatribes against "the feeling of guilt" that some people think they are obliged to derive from such explanations, will not prevail against this boon.

---

[1] "Already you are beginning to be enlightened, because there is admission of guilt within you."

Cynicism is the reverse side of hypocrisy. It does not give the truth about man.

History consumes, like psychology.

. . . He is not an extremist, nor a biased man. He is a wise man, fair. He is wary of all passion. Moreover, he has experience, he knows that in all matters there is wrong on both sides and that nothing is to be gained by looking too closely. He knows too that you have to live and that life is impossible without mutual concessions and a certain "happy medium". In all controversies he suffers at seeing two men "attacking one another". It is also one of his maxims that there is always a risk in running foul of any accepted opinion whatever. Therefore people often have recourse to his arbitration. Of two adversaries who take him to witness, if one says that two and two make five, and the other that they make four, he prudently inclines towards the middle solution: two and two, he suggests, more or less make four and a half.

It is not sincerity, it is Truth which frees us. Now it only frees us because it transforms us. It tears us away from our inmost slavery. To seek sincerity above all things is perhaps, at bottom, not to want to be transformed; it is to cling to yourself, to have a morbid love of yourself, just as your are, that is to say, false. It is to refuse release.

Omnis homo mendax. One can only *pray* for sincerity.

"Lying is a vice only when it does harm; it is a very great virtue when it does good." If the man to whom that maxim is attributed really wrote it, at least he had the face to do so. There are others who put it into practice and will never confess it, even in secret.

"O falsehood, falsehood, wherever we are!" (KIERKEGAARD).

Nothing is harder to defend against the suspicion of hypocrisy than uprightness. Those who have not got it are unable to imagine it in others. Those who have it are not sufficiently calculating to foresee resentment or clever enough to guard against it. Soon everything becomes a disquieting sign to their disadvantage, and the very absence of any sign becomes the most irritating, the gravest, of all signs.

When crassness reaches a certain point, we must no longer say: "Pharisee", but "Philistine". . . .

"The Pilgrim of the Absolute" is a fine title. But care must be taken to preserve its correct value for the first substantive, as well as for the second.

Psychologists assure us that it is our own short-comings especially that we hate in other people. That is very possible, and is even a matter of quite common experience. But, on the other hand, we are also capable of especially appreciating in others the good qualities we most lack. No doubt to do that we must bear in our own selves at least "the seed and the root" (FR. TOURNEMINE).[2] But in each of us, how many seeds there are that have not come up, how many roots without stems!

If we do not hope for what cannot be hoped for, we shall not recognize it (HERACLITUS in Clement, *Stromata*, ii, 4, 17, 1).

"It is odd! I have always thought that the moral value of any being is proved, not by what he demands from others, but by what he does himself" (z . . . , representing Vladimir Soloviev, in *Three Conversations*).

It not infrequently happens that we have the highest opinion of those good qualities in which we

[2] The French Jesuit of the eighteenth century, editor of the *Journal de Trévoux*. He was an admirer of Fénelon and edited his *Traité de l'existence et des attributs de Dieu*.

are most wanting. It is also what we should be most incapable of doing ourselves that we sometimes appreciate more than anything. Everyone has his job, which is a limiting factor; his temperament, which he can scarcely change. Everyone has his style, as he has his particular skill. It does not follow from that that he puts forward his style as a model, or that he places the object of his proficiency above every other object. One may go farther; in our freedom in the choice of subject, it happens that we may avoid those we have most at heart; or else we give them up after the first attempts. The urge is countered by a sort of modesty and we are deterred from continuing. We feel we are not up to it. We make a few circles round it, clear a few approaches, at the most lop a few small branches off the trunk, knock a few chips off the intact block. We know before we start that we shall leave the essential unsaid.

"The worst weakness of our minds is our failure to be aware of the greatest problems, because they are presented in the form of what is nearest to us"[3] (PIERRE TEILHARD DE CHARDIN).

[3] Jesuit theologian, scientist and philosopher (1881–1955). His influence on French Catholic thought has increased in the

If there be no man without humanity, much less still is there any Humanity without men.

By calling us back inwards, the Gospel is at the same time calling us back to the truth of human relationships, that truth fatally betrayed by all ideologies and political systems.

Among philosophers there are some who do not want to see the problems of existence: witness a whole genealogical tree of rationalists. There are some who simply declare such problems to be already solved; such is the whole spiritual family that has a so-called "mystical" tendency. Then there are some who do not want to have any solutions for them; such are many agnostics and also numerous existentialists who make this decision as a matter of principle. There are some who want to solve these problems only with the tools

_____

last few years and a number of works on his thought have recently been published. After teaching in Peking and at the Institut Catholique in Paris, he became head of the geological department at the Ecole Pratique des Hautes Etudes, investigating the origins of man. He was elected to the Académie des Sciences in 1950.

of reason. And there are some who, out of sheer despair of reason, blithely impute to it what they take to be faith. Finally, there are some who see and admit that what is involved here is more than just great problems. With them reason can do its proper work; but from the bottom of their hearts the cry always explodes: "I stretch out my arms to my Deliverer."

Why be astonished at seeing so many men indifferent to the demands of the pure idea of Truth, when we see so many equally blind to all radiance of Beauty?

Elementary things are also essential things. Instead of abandoning them as banalities so as to chase after subtle novelties, we must always go back to them, to go into them more deeply.

There is no need to be a believer to revolt against the abuses men suffer from. Or to contrive to suppress them or get rid of them one by one. But faith alone will take man into a new domain, where the source of abuses is dried up.

"No man is a great man to his valet." That is meant to be a criticism of the "great man". It may be as well, and especially so, a criticism of the "valet". And the person who minted that maxim no doubt took less after the "great man" than the "valet".

It is above all, and expressly, to knowledge in religious matters, that we must apply Bossuet's exclamation: "Woe to knowledge which does not lead to love!" A fig for those reflections, discussions, studies, which tend, as Fénelon used to say, "only to make men philosophize on Christianity and not to make them Christians!"

"This world will end as it wills to do", Renouvier used to say.[4] The fortunes of Catholicism, we

[4] Charles-Bernard Renouvier (1815–1903) is commonly regarded as a neo-Kantian philosopher. His philosophy

shall say likewise, will depend, in future generations, on what we shall have willed them to be. It
is right to listen to the lessons of sociology and to
pay heed to the great laws of historical development—but only on condition of reacting to them.
Otherwise, it would be letting ourselves be
caught in the trap. "Every action", said Blondel,
"is a turning-point in the history of the universe."

For lack of a mirror, you cannot see your face. For
lack of adversaries, you do not know your fail-
ings[5] (NICHIREN, *Kaimokusho,* c, v. VII).

"People ought not to think so much about what
they have *to do;* they ought rather to consider
what they should *be.*" That reflection of Meister
Eckhart's should not hinder action, but the man

---

makes an original synthesis of that of Comte as well as Kant,
though modifying elements of both. The most important of
his many works are the four *Essais de Critique générale* (1854–
64), though no doubt his books on Victor Hugo have been
more widely read.

[5] The Japanese Buddhist monk of the thirteenth century.

of action more than any other should make it his own.

True perspicacity is always naïve.

It is lightly said of certain men that they were ineffective. Yet they had the finest sort of effectiveness. They preserved human delicacy, human nobility. . . . And those things are not preserved by themselves.

Have not other kinds of effectiveness, of which too much is heard, consisted above all in dehumanizing us?

When we choose the poor, we can always be sure of not going wrong. When we choose an ideology, we can never be sure of not being at least partly wrong.

When we have complied with an ideology, we can never be sure of having taken the right course. When we choose the poor, we are always sure, doubly sure, of having made a good choice. We have chosen like Jesus. And we have chosen Jesus.

Taking sides is one thing, committing ourselves is another. The first may involve violence, and remain superficial. The second, on the contrary, is a decision made in the depths of our being, and the positive is so dominant an element, that often we are not even involved in any opposition.

Pamphleteering, caricature, crude popularization, political manoeuvring, arrogance, and brutality taking the place of proof, offensive innuendos, cheap store psycho-analysis: all that is readily decked out today with the fine name of "committed philosophy".

Nothing is more ingenious, more obstinate, nastier—indeed, in a sense, more clear sighted, than mediocrity harrying every form of superiority that offends it.

If man could enter inside himself and have a vision of himself both penetrating and sincere,

simple and straightforward, he would no longer
dare to take refuge in all the alibis of psychological and sociological analysis. He would no longer
dare to imagine that anything, which is not the
changing of his heart by a Stronger than he, can
ever free him.

There is nothing more demanding than the taste
for mediocrity. Beneath its ever moderate appearance there is nothing more intemperate;
nothing surer in its instinct; nothing more pitiless
in its refusals. It suffers no greatness, shows
beauty no mercy.

It is a great illusion to confuse desire and love,
need and charity (*eros* and *agape*). It is one scarcely
less great to believe that our love of God can and
must break radically away from our condition as a
creature, or that in the least of our natural loves, if
it rise to the human, there is not something there
already which from afar relates it to charity. The
fundamental optimism of the Thomist and of the
Salesian doctrine seems in this connection the
only true one, the only one worthy of man, the
only one as well which fully satisfies the data of

Revelation. And, still following revealed data, we may carry reflection on the consequences of sin very far, without for that reason departing from Revelation. . . . *Signatum est super nos lumen vultus tui, Domine!*[6]

Many are the frightful things, but nothing
Is more frightful than man.

(SOPHOCLES, Antigone)

Why must we always complain about the weight of the elements and the aridity of the desert? Should we not rather admire the fertile oases and the blades of grass thrusting up? If you object that grass is too infrequent and the desert too big, then my answer is that that is very true and all the more matter for admiration. In life it is always the improbable that happens, the unexpected miracle that takes place. We can take it for granted that man is a heavy opaque creature, whose wells are all blocked, and that we can expect nothing from him. Yet, all the same, here is the miracle happen-

---

[6] ". . . But already, Lord, the sun of thy favour shines out clear above us", Psalm iv, 7 (Knox).

ing. In the midst of that heavy and rocky stretch, there in that little point yonder, is water seeping, grass thrusting up.

The one law, too natural a thing; the other, the exception, wonderful.

. . . And, if we look properly, the exceptions increase. Everywhere, across the desert, you can see the greenness of oases appearing. . . .

XI

World

⚜

Paul has said: "A Greek with the Greeks, a Jew with the Jews." He did not say: "An anti-Jew with the Greeks, an anti-Greek with the Jews." He said: "I have become all things to all men," and not: "I have taken on the prejudices and passions of all." He said: "In order to win them over to Christ", and not: "In order to let myself be won over to their human standpoints." In any event, what he said was: "A Greek with the Greeks, a Jew with the Jews", and this is the complete opposite of a scornful indifference which changes its speech and its appearance according to situation and cirumstance and never really comes into full communion with men, whom one has accepted only from the outside. This, however, is what the

Apostle intends, an imitation of Jesus, of whom it is said: "In him was only Yes."

"Evil in the world is the slave who draws the water up" (CLAUDEL). "Felix culpa!" chants also the Catholic Church. Which does not mean that evil does not remain evil.

May the man who is learned and wise, really learned and wise, not make hard-and-fast judgments! May he not believe that he contains all truth and justice in himself because his doctrine is infallible and his formulas correct! May his knowledge and his wisdom proclaim aloud to him their inadequacy! May he remain open to the restless spirit of those who are seeking, and to the confused appeals of those who are troubled! Above all, may he consent to be taught by the man who puts his charity into effect, whatever be the deficiencies of his language or however far his ideas may seem to stray! May he, instead of first judging, condemning his brother, get ready to collaborate, and in this work of collaboration, which may be difficult, may he be persuaded that it is not from him, the learned and wise, even if there must be much discussion, much rectification, that the better part will come!

May we be preserved from a nature fully humanized at last—supposing that were possible—if the result or condition of it were to be a man fully naturalized!

It might be thought that by establishing the distinction between the spiritual and the temporal, between religion and politics, between the salvation of the soul and the interests of the city, the Gospel provided a principle that led away from social action. It is the contrary that has happened, and logically so. For, by releasing the germ of spiritual freedom that is deep within each individual, that distinction forces us to see in him, no longer merely the subject who must be used in the building of an empire or the citizen who must play his part inside the city, but the personal being in whose cause we must be interested. The Gospel had to make us, as it were, come unstuck from the earth, to make something emerge in us which escapes the earth, so that interest in the social problem might itself break free from that interest in the city and its cohesion which led sway in the ancient world. And so that the latter does not again absorb the former, always a risk, fidelity to the Gospel must preserve in us what has emerged.

No longer to believe, in fact, in the assimilating and transforming power of Christianity; to divert the exercise of Christian prudence so as to make of it an entirely negative and defensive prudential system: such is one of the most fatal forms of lack of faith. It is to believe no longer, in fact, in Christian vitality. It is to refuse confidence in the Holy Spirit. It is to justify as if on principle those who think that Christianity has grown old for good.

Our faith, thank God, is not touched. It remains solid in itself. But does it not too often happen that we no longer have *faith in our faith?* That perhaps is the great ill, the alarming sign of a lessening of our stamina, one of the main causes of our weakness. That is what makes us, not frankly greet the truth that may be found outside, but for ever be filled with fear, and hobble, blush and squint.

144

Everywhere we must fight, fight in earnest—and everywhere we must dread victory.

Till the last day—and it is a good thing—the Church will be "militant". Inside as outside, each of us must always be at strife, and each of our successors as well, indefinitely, like ourselves.

Christianity is not one of the great things of history: it is history which is one of the great things of Christianity.

We must not set up the Prophets who heralded him against Jesus himself. We must not pervert the Old Testament by using it against the New. We must not resume the old messianic attitude by giving the Old Testament a sense against which Jesus protested.

Nothing is more wonderful, in the reality of things, than the way the two Testaments hinge on one another. But neither is there anything trickier than the accurate perception of such a fact.

Christian Tradition has been meditating on this for two thousand years and will go on doing so. It will go on, from one age to another, finding in it the mainspring of a solution for the most contemporary and seemingly unknown problems.

"Man is made in the image of God, and whatever, instead of leading him back to that image, leads him away from it, whether it is a question of his pleasure or his work, of his ideas or his passions, that is 'escapism!' "[1] (LOUIS BOUYER) "Conditions d'une prédication pastorale", *La Maison Dieu,* 39, p. 57).

When you reproach Jesus with still having left room for Caesar, instead of claiming all for "God", you are getting ready, without seeing it, to give yourself all the room or to let Caesar have it soon. People reproach Jesus with only half freeing man and, moving away from Jesus, they are already bringing man back inevitably to the way of slavery.

[1] Certain of the works of this Oratorian (b. 1913), a convert from Protestantism, have been translated into English, e.g., *The Paschal Mystery* (Unwin, 1951); *The Meaning of the Monastic Life* (Burns and Oates, 1955); *Woman and the Church* (Ignatius, 1979).

Events are constantly pointing this out.

"Christ", proclaims Gorki through the voice of one of his characters, "lacked steadfastness. 'May this cup pass away from me', he said. And *he recognized Caesar.* God cannot recognize the power of one man over others, he who is all power! He does not divide his soul: this is God's, and that is man's. . . ."

"He recognized Caesar. . . ." But those who find that concession excessive are not long in confusing Caesar with God.

For a Catholic, being a "militant", as they say, is not without its dangers. For, apart from the interior battles which one must wage against oneself, how could one fight without fighting *against* someone? How could one then not fail in equanimity, love, patience, humility, even justice and other virtues, without which one cannot be a true Catholic, much less *a fortiori* a truly "militant Catholic"?

We must not be impatient. We must not want to achieve unity too cheaply. That would be to obtain merely a debased unity, even under the guise of unanimous charity.

The craftsman respects the resistance of matter; he knows he would gain nothing by "forcing". Still more is it necessary to respect the resistance of persons. Better an order which is less easy, a less coherent universe, a more arduous harmony, a slower building up, than success which, though better in appearance, is secured at the price of stifling what is best.

If you are not yourself in a position to profit from injustice and if you do not have to make any effort to overcome this temptation, you must show complete moderation in your manner of fighting injustice in others. It is important not to forget, too, that many who protest in the name of justice would only like—in good faith perhaps—to be the strongest and most favored themselves.

One of the worst betrayals of the Gospel: under the guise of charity, to cover and consummate injustice.

Like those diseases whose development is related to surrounding conditions, which craftily contend with the remedy and reappear in another form as soon as they are thought to have been vanquished, so does the radical ill that man bears deep within himself come to the surface again in unforeseeable forms at each transformation of society.

A man may find the most truly human happiness through a meditation on the Apocalypse rather than through an analysis by Marx or anyone else.

Let us not draw from that, it must be added, the conclusion that meditation can take the place of all analysis. . . .

Work: begot in man by an animal need, and, at the same time, a tool by which to lift himself above animality. A hard bondage and a liberating force. Today still it remains marked by this ambiguous character.

The more it will be shown that work ought not to be a penalty—and that there is something offensive to man in formulating a theory of work which considers it as essentially a penalty—the more, for this very reason, that penal quality will appear—a penal quality which from many points of view is too much a characteristic of it, and which one cannot see that it will ever cease entirely to have.

"That ought not to be": is not that in fact the judgment found at the bottom of all *human* suffering?

The fact that we recognize that work may have a punitive character, which indeed the Latin word *labor* implies, does not mean that we may define work in that way. On the contrary, the idea of punishment is absent from the definition of the word. So, our recognition of this punitive aspect must not deter us from working out a system which shows not only the necessity of work and all the objective advantages accruing from it, but, what is more essential, the nobility and the humanizing value that it has. Neither must this recognition discourage us from seeking the best conditions in which this humanizing value may acquire its full effectiveness. Rather does it compel us to do this.

To try to justify a view of society in which work bears a punitive character would be pure sophistry, or rather a twofold sophistry; for the existence of this punitive quality is a scandalous fact and is valid in any case only in the realm of the spirit—and, what is more, even in that realm its validity is dependent upon the seeming lack of justification for it, on its being a scandalous fact, not an accepted matter of course.

"There will always be the sick": that is not an invitation to close down Medical Faculties; on the contrary! "The poor you will always have with you": that does not deprive us of arms in our fight against pauperism; on the contrary! The same here.

Shall I refuse my brother a glass of water, telling him that I am fully occupied in recovering the meaning of God?

"All the consequences of the Gospel!"—Yes, but, first, all its substance. All its demands. Or, more modestly: the letter of it.

If not, I am afraid that the chase after consequences is in reality flight; that the so-called completeness is a betrayal; that in forgetfulness of the original word the spirit is lost.

The gleams of light the Gospel indirectly casts illuminate vast human planes, the size of the globe and of history. But, meanwhile, every day, in its direct light, may it be for each of us what the Psalm says: *lucerna pedibus meis et lumen semitis meis*.[2]

At each sincere stirring of charity, the Gospel triumphs, Christianity is already effective.

We must seek the realization of Christianity in society in order to be faithful to the Gospel—and not make use of the Gospel in order to achieve Christianity in society. The latter attitude would pervert the Gospel by reducing it to the role of a means, whilst the former is imperative, whatever the apparent consequences. Alone it respects the absoluteness of the Gospel.

We do not know what the social realization of the Gospel might be; but, however desirable this

[2] "Thy word is a lamp to my feet, and a light to my paths", Psalm cxviii, 105 (Douai Version).

may seem to us, we know in advance that Christianity cannot be enclosed within it.

The social accomplishment of the Gospel is one thing, and life according to the Gospel another. Never will the former, whatever stage it reach, dispense us from the latter, or bring it about spontaneously; and the latter does not have to wait for the former to become active and flourish.

All things are corrupted by desire of success. You want to "bring it off", show results, have an effect on opinion, count for something. . . . And you get impatient and disdain action that is hidden, and gradually you assume, with the world's methods, the spirit of the world. And you end by making a little noise—which goes with the wind.

As man had once to free himself from the contemplation of the world, without ceasing on that account to be filled with wonder at this world which is the work of God, so must he now free himself from the manufacture of the world, without ceasing to pursue in it the work that God entrusts to him. That is the price of Christian hope, as it was once that of faith.

As Christians of former ages plunged into the contemplation of the world so that they might, while gaining support from this contemplation, yet free themselves from it and so rise up to God, so must we today plunge into history so as to free ourselves from it and rest in the bosom of God.

No "emergency order" could take our attention away for long from any essential task. Never can we consent to the crushing of men by want. Never can we wait for all to be well on this earth to call man back to himself. And in many cases we must recognize that it is not want in another that causes our failure here: it is our own want, our want of faith.

In the search for Christian unity, the process is not at all the same as in diplomatic negotiations or political deals. If these latter do not end in some formula of agreement, they have achieved nothing. In the spiritual realm, on the other hand, every effort bears in itself its own effectiveness.

Every earnest, willing of union is a real step towards union. And even supposing that the latter, in its complete form, must for ever elude us, even become ever more improbable, each step towards it nevertheless constitutes an absolute gain. It is an admirable paradox! Every disposition toward union brings it effectively nearer, because it increases charity, which is in itself a unifying factor.

He who has not as much and more real pity, really charitable pity, for the spiritual want of so many wealthy people, than for the material want of the poor, has not the feelings of a Christian in him. But the first of these two forms of pity cannot be a pretext for him to rid himself of the other one.

"Never speak of God from memory, never speak of him as of someone absent" (MAURICE BLONDEL).

The apostle who elects to be faithful to the Gospel will always find himself caught, in the very midst of his own people, between two lines of adversaries: those who judge him to be ineffective because he does not consent to betray his mission so as to devote himself to temporal tasks and forms of propaganda and those who see in him a disturber, because instead of maintaining them in a state of satisfaction with themselves, he is forever giving them a troubled conscience.

Why should he be surprised? Electing to conform to the spirit of Jesus, he accepted beforehand to be judged and treated like him. What Pascal said of Jesus and his preaching is made new in every age: "To that all men are opposed."

XII

Others

To differ, even deeply, one from another, is not to be enemies: it is simply to be. To recognize and accept one's own difference is not pride. To recognize and accept the difference of others is not weakness. If union has to be, if union offers any meaning at all, it must be union between different men. And it is above all in the recognition and acceptance of difference that difference is overcome and union achieved.

We would be more indulgent with one another, indeed, we would have more mutual love and admiration, if from early on were inculcated in us the principle of the division of labor and all its consequences: division of talents, of tastes, of vocations, of orientations, of habits and all sorts of other qualities. Dialogue among us would not then be less serious, rather more peaceful. Spontaneously we would then make efforts to reach a common goal. We would then see that the Creator's gifts to human nature are in practice irreconcilable in individual members of the human race. And we would find beauty in this in spite of all the questions, uncertainties, mutual difficulties and conflicts involved, because we would also have mutual respect and trust with an eye to a richer, subtler, and really rewarding harmony.

Would not the setting aside of all prejudice come in the end to the giving up of all difference? Would not a mankind where there reigned a full and total understanding by everyone of each other be mankind brought down to the level of the herd?

Never will men understand one another. Even where a fundamental agreement holds sway uncontested, what lacerations yet remain! What active divergences of mind, soul, and temperament! What obscurities, suddenly seen to be fraught with menace, even in the relationships of those most united in heart!

Everywhere the only possible solution to the

problem of life in common and of the peaceful intercourse of minds is no doubt a temporary solution, an ever uncertain balance between antagonistic forces or thoughts. Thrusts in opposite directions must be organized to prevent their becoming violent and reckless blows: they must be brought into equilibrium, into harmony, if it is possible. This is tricky work, always to be done again, or at least completed. But let us beware of constantly wishing to suppress these thrusts: otherwise, everything would return to the undifferentiated state, to dust, to nothingness.

If this view contains at least a portion of truth, that is enough to provide us with abundant consolation for much painful oppositon.

By calling us within ourselves the Gospel refers us continually to the truth of human relationships, that truth which is betrayed with ominous necessity by all ideologies and political undertakings.

Should we always presume that to human thoughts and works the same applies as to the basket in which one rotten fruit is enough to spoil the whole bunch? Why should the faulty element in a thought always be the dominant and virulent one, which tomorrow will draw all others in its direction? Why don't we ever believe in the power of the true and the good, in a possible restoration, indeed, in the profound transformation and "conversion" that the lesser parts may undergo under the influence of the better? Francis de Sales stated: "All the defects of a good work cannot vitiate its essential goodness."

To accuse of egoism certain people who seem to think only of themselves is to be lacking in charity. Perhaps they are merely faithful to a duty towards themselves which is for them the first form of their duty towards their neighbor. Perhaps they have an imperious need to seek and express themselves. Perhaps they forget themselves better like this, escape better from their egotistic selves, than in active tasks, seemingly more disinterested. Perhaps they have a mission to bring to light some dark element, which, in the depths of themselves, demands to be born, and which is to become the good of everyone.

Without a number of these seeming egoists, how poverty-stricken humanity would be!

Most of the time men are so evil towards one another because at bottom they are afraid of one another.

We think we can affirm that tolerance is making progress. What we don't realize is that a new intolerance has taken the place of the old one.

They are most zealous to caricature: they must fabricate the object they criticize; they must be able to mock it and denounce it. Then comes the zeal for rejection: every explanation that could possibly restore the true meaning of the object must be invalidated.

A vulgarity that disfigures and vilifies, political intrigues and machinations, presumption instead of proofs, unfriendly innuendoes, psychoanalytical amenities: all of this claims for itself today the noble title of *philosophie engagée.* . . .

161

However urgent what is social may be, we must always preserve the primacy of what is human in ourselves. For the social will not thereby be neglected: it is contained in the human. But the human might be excluded from the social, sacrificed to the social, and in that case the social itself would lose its value. It would not be long before it again became what it used to be. It would be nothing but a new Moloch.

Man does not live on bread alone. The spirit does not wait, cannot wait. Hunger of the soul is as brutal as that of the body. It is as fatal. Only, if you are already paying little attention to those dying of bodily hunger, those who are dying of spiritual hunger will attract no attention.

Two symmetrical illusions, one as deadly as the other: counting on verbal persuasion to secure the practice of justice—counting on the force of the law to found the reign of charity.

Man is fine when he works and fights for fine causes. But if he at last achieved victory, would he be fine any longer?

History is a perpetual disappointment—and it is forever achieving utopias.

The Marxist fighter in the heart of capitalist society is held up for my admiration. I admire him; moreover, I can recognize in him many human features which owe nothing to Marxism, and I also find a few distortions which are due to it. What interests me more, in any case, so as to know if I must follow this man in his struggle or only try to imitate his virtues, is to have some idea of the final result, that is to say, of the man submissive and satisfied in the heart of Marxist society. Now, I can see that man quite altered and not so fine.

Even if man's happiness can be looked for in the future, his dignity can be respected only in the present. In conflicting circumstances one must choose dignity before happiness, both for oneself and for others. Only in this way can both be safeguarded at once.

Rare are the men who rise high enough to glimpse the fact that, if you do not adopt all their partial views, it is most certainly not because you adopt the opposite ones. Rare are they who, not seeing you in their camp, do not suppose that you are hedged in by the one opposite, who do not take concern for justice for some unacknowledged complicity. All the big words of our time do not make it a fact that we are habitually freed from the group or clan mentality.

As soon as charity becomes technically organized,[1] it can no longer be certain—except in some

---

[1] The reference is to certain social developments in France since the Second World War.

very simple, very elementary, undertakings—of attaining its aim. In two equally charitable persons it may follow two opposite courses. Here they are, henceforth, confronting one another. They are tempted to forget what they ultimately will and what first inspired them, which are the same in both cases, in favor of their now divergent objectives. Countless clashes of interest arise. . . . If you now but go so far as to make sacred the means employed instead of the end in view, you have the frightful emergence of sectarianism, which gives rise to further ills. All the harshness of spiritual struggles—without their nobility. The man who decides in favor of another technique is quickly accused of yielding to base feelings, or of playing into the hands of men with base feelings, etc. Soon every means will be judged good to bring him down. At all cost the coming of the reign of charity must be ensured, according to the plan that has been conceived, considered as the only one effective. This plan must succeed, the good cause triumph. The masses must be won over to it. It must be imposed on the refractory.

Indeed, they carry the day, victory is there. But is it the victory of charity? One would like to believe it: technically organized charity, it is said, has become effective. Yes, but a twofold misfortune has occurred on the way: it has ceased to be charitable, and the effectiveness which it is fondly thought has been achieved is no longer the same as that in question at the start. The object at first expected has not been attained. Has it even been approached? All that has been done is to conquer a position that they would like to think "inter-mediary", rather in the manner of that revolution which has set up the "dictatorship of the pro-letariat"—in fact, a totalitarian form of State—when the revolutionaries set their hopes on the advent of a stateless society.

. . . And that is not to say that charity must not become technically organized. But the risks must be seriously envisaged. May charity see that it does not let fall the modest prey for the vast shadow! May its present action, real, immediate, day after day, not be sacrificed for the dream of its future! May charity, on becoming technically or-ganized, undertake to remain charity, first and foremost and forever!

May the new designation not be allowed to corrode the old one! May the lining not consume the material!

Many people always see only the disadvantages of the present state of affairs and only the advantages of the one that ought to replace it. What is more, they think that all you have to do is destroy what exists and The Ideal will at once arise from its ruins—and they don't give a thought to how this might occur. Anyone who shows himself ready to offer practical help to the present reality, with all its defects, is defamed for supporting injustice, for opposing the kingdom of justice.

Oh, how unfortunate it is to be too right, when you are only right negatively! Oh, how bad it is to have good principles, when your heart is not open to the sweetness and humility of Christ! Oh, how sad it is to triumph, when you see your brother tripping over the stumbling-block! Oh, how fatal it is to be in favor at court, when you nourish in yourself the court spirit!

More to be pitied than all the unfortunates are these triumphers, these doctrinaires, these fine reasoners, these court favorites! Who will take them the Gospel?

When we are right without praying, without loving, our "right" bears but the fruits of death. To be right against everyone else is too cheap a thing and often also too seductive.

A false prophet is not one who predicts false things, but one whose guiding principle is not the true, one who has an ear more to the world than to God, who fondles the spirit of the age— whether it is embodied in the "princes", the "influential" or the "mass". He takes up the cause of generous ideas just when these are beginning to rot; he enters the field of action just at the moment when such engagement promises more advantages than dangers. He does not always do what is evil, but his activity is, at the very least, full of vanity. This often discourages the person who can glimpse the impending disaster from agreeing with him. And he always conspires against the true prophets.

Religion, especially the Christian religion, is accused of engendering fanaticism. There has, of course, been fanaticism among Christians, otherwise they would not have been human. But it is precisely authentic, logical and interiorly lived faith that preserves one from all fanaticism. Nonreligious, purely worldly man, on the other hand, can hardly escape it without falling prey to the opposite danger: egotistic skepticism.

We fail against love of neighbor when we let spoil in ourselves the sole treasure we are in a position of transmitting to men: faith, hope, love for Christ. If we want to preserve this treasure and make it bear fruit both within and outside ourselves, then the more we are open to the plight and needs of our time, the more traditional must we be in the religious sphere.

To love one's neighbor in God is to love him in his vocation, in the call of God which constitutes him. It is therefore to love him in the way he is most himself; to love him with the only love which, reaching beyond those "qualities" of which Pascal wrote, touches him in his most vivid and irreducible particularity. It is to love him in the love of God which causes him to be and to be such as he is, which confers on him that unique essential personality which Pascal said he sought without finding—which is in fact not found so long as we do not love God.

And it is at the same time to love him with a love which remains universal—because the vocation which is peculiarly his is always inscribed in the heart of the great common vocation, with the great unanimous concert in view.

XIII

Suffering

As their refinement and humaneness increase, men invent more and more new ways of making one another suffer—or of tormenting themselves. So, always, is suffering reborn, keener still, from all that tends to extirpate it.

All suffering is unique—and all suffering is common. I have to be reminded of the latter truth when I am suffering myself—and of the former when I see others suffering.

The agony of suffering: a word doubly accurate, in the sense of death and in the sense of struggle.

The adversary's lance goes through to the heart. It pierces the heart. And, paradoxically, the struggle consists in not thrusting away the point. It consists in opening the heart, so that the point is sure to reach it. *Fiat:* the supreme activity, consent to death. Then suffering accomplishes its work. The burning point in the depth of one's being consumes that part which must die.

To welcome suffering is not to take pleasure in it. It is not love of suffering for its own sake. It is consent to one's humiliation by it. It is the opening of one's self to the blessings of what is inevitable, like earth which allows the water of heaven to soak right through it.

There is an art in suffering—but it must not be confused either with the art of cultivating suffering or with the art of avoiding it.

He who takes pity on himself and is moved by his own pain, at once loses the boon it offers. Likewise, he who withdraws within it and takes perverse pleasure in savoring the bitterness of it.

When suffering forces itself upon us, we must neither repel it nor yield to it. We must neither fight nor trick it. We must welcome it without indulging ourselves. But such a welcome is never final. It constitutes, therefore, the highest exercise of freedom.

The value pain has is the value joy has. They are two correlatives, and more than correlatives. Pain is the reverse side of that unique fabric which, on its proper side, is—or will be—joy. But we must first accept the reverse side, which is the only one offered us, without wanting to turn the fabric— for that is impossible—without yet knowing the proper side. Under the species of pain, the substance of joy is there, already. That is what will appear one day.

And does not the believer, fortified by the Promise of Christ, sometimes have a presentiment of it, already?

There is one way only of being happy: not to be ignorant of suffering, and not to run away from it; but to accept the transfiguration it brings. *Tristitia vestra vertetur in gaudium.*[1]

[1] "But your distress shall be turned to joy", John xvi, 20 (Knox).

True happiness can only be the result of an alchemy.

When pain is at its height, to escape the poison it distils, look at yourself now and again with a humorous eye. Believe me, that remedy is more effective than any heroic fight. It is easier as well, if you are at all alive, in the ordinary course of things, to the human comedy—without excluding yourself from it.

"If your soul is troubled, go to church, kneel and pray."

"If your soul is still troubled, go find your confessor, sit at his feet and open your soul to him.

"And if your soul remains troubled, then, withdraw to your cell, lie down on your mattress, *and sleep.*"

All pain is obscure: as soon as you see the meaning of it, it vanishes. But deep pain is more than obscure: it is a pulling of ourselves apart, a contradiction which is lived; therefore it leaves us no rest and seems to allow us no acquiescence. We can accept night. We cannot fail to struggle with contradiction.

When pain desires to take possession of a soul, it attacks on all fronts at once, and its armies force their way by a converging manoeuvre right into the center.

When you think you have at last driven that wild beast out, you come across it again crouching in a dark corner of the dwelling, ready to spring anew on to its prey.

When we really suffer, we always suffer badly.

The treatment of suffering demands great simplicity. We must neither flee from it nor harbor it. We must love it without indulging ourselves in it. We must dominate it without pride.

We must believe in the blessing it brings and let it have its way, without ceasing to deem it bad.

It is an illusion to think that, to accept suffering, it is enough to be passive. Or rather, there is nothing more active than this passivity. It can only be the fruit of struggle. Supreme suffering is the supreme fight: *agony*.

He who takes himself too seriously will never dominate his pain. It is his pain that dominates him, even if he seems to have got the better of it. It puts a strain on him, hardens him, withers him. It imposes a stern philosophy on him. In the finest realization of his type, the stoic is not a completely free man.

Disappointment is a deadly enemy. It begets the temptation of sadness and of contempt. The highest victory is to preserve, in spite of it, one's early freshness and joy.

Disappointment is not only a bitter potion: it is poison—which it is not in our power to refuse. But this poison can be overcome.

Together with prayer and love, suffering is one of the three ways which free us from sentimentality. Strictly speaking, these three ways combine so as to make only one. For we cannot truly gain entry to prayer or love without suffering, and love remains closed to whoever does not implore it.

But the way which frees us from sentimentality is also that which leads to the deep springs that nourish the affections.

There are elementary sufferings, and there are some that can be called luxury sufferings. But such a distinction really makes sense only for the person looking from the outside. No real suffering, at the moment it is experienced, is noble.

It is not always a good thing to take refuge too soon in the Bosom of God. This running away may conceal a secret pride, or the avid search for an anaesthetic. The person who suffers has the finest opportunity of bringing the law of Christian life into effect: let him not be ashamed of resembling and having recourse to the Man of Sorrows.

Suffering is not imaginary, even when it is imagination causing the suffering. But one may be responsible for the state of one's imagination.

Suffering is never confined within the moment. It is never simply undergone. Like everything else in the life of one's conscious self it is not only always felt, but actually discerned; that is to say, positively built up. It is always memory and anticipation. That is verifiable even in the humblest suffering of the body.

Instantaneous pain, which is that which animals undergo, is so different from human pain, that no doubt it does not deserve this same name of suffering. Animals do not really suffer, because they do not make themselves suffer. They do not add the twofold reaction of memory and anticipation to the shock they undergo. Here, as everywhere else, the greatness of man brings about his wretchedness.

Must we seek to guard against suffering by striving to live only in the instant? That is possible, to a certain extent, only in bodily pain—and sometimes nature is a party to this herself. Animal pain brings man down to animal life, thus creating, in a certain measure, its own anaesthetic. But when it is a matter of human pain, such a recipe is unworthy of man.

"Sufficient for the day is the evil thereof." Yet it is neither possible nor desirable wholly to escape memory or anticipation. It is neither possible nor desirable to take refuge in the dimensionless animal moment. But man spontaneously poisons his suffering by living his memories in resentment and his anticipations in fear and anxiety.[2] The art of suffering is in a large measure the art of making the past and the future healthy as they are being lived in the instant of pain. Without suppressing the two dimensions which give it body, it is a question, then, of rightly disposing the content. Resentment is to become adhesion, and fear turn into hope. For that to be, pain must be lived in the Present of God.

Then suffering is not removed, but it has lost its venom. It no longer poisons the soul: on the

[2] This can be verified even in the most banal case: the injured person on a hospital bed who chews over in his mind "the stupid accident" of which he was a victim and who is scared of future difficulties. (Author's note.)

contrary, it purifies it. It is a bearer not of anguish any more, but of peace.

Tranquillus Deus tranquillat omnia, et quietum aspicere, quiescere est[3] (ST. BERNARD).

"The only thing left to do is to suffer": it is soon said; it is ill said. It is a fallacious promise of rest. Never is there only suffering left, if by that is meant pure passivity, a justifiable surrender. The reception of suffering is active passivity, and all the problems of action are there met with again, more inward and more subtle.

Man may be divided, torn, unbalanced even: should one call him happy if he were not?

Every age has always been the worst—and if there were some which were really the worst, it was those which gave birth to the greatest things.

---

[3] "God in his peace stills all things, and to behold him at rest, is to be at rest ourselves."

St. Augustine, by whose light we are still illuminated, was, in his last years, a petty bishop besieged by the Barbarians; he saw the crumbling of the great empire whose history seemed to be identified with that of the world. . . . It was in the sixth century, "an age of perpetual tribulation and threats", when Italy was in the hands of the Goths and Lombards, that wonderful thing, the Roman Liturgy, was most enriched. In the middle of the thirteenth century, that great century of Christendom, the greatest, the only one, the one that awakens so much nostalgia, the one that will never come back, Christendom thought its last hour had come. No cry of distress is comparable, perhaps, to the speech given in 1245 by Pope Innocent IV at Lyon, in the refectory of Saint-Just: the abominable morals of prelates and faithful, the insolence of the Saracens, the schism of the Greeks, the brutality of the Tartars, the persecutions by an impious emperor. . . . Such are the five wounds of which the Church is dying: to save the little that can be saved, let every one dig trenches, the only recourse against the Tartars. . . .

"This century is a century of iron!" wailed Marsiglio Ficino, in the fifteenth century, at Florence!

Is there not enough in all that to give us courage?

There will always be something to wail over and something to weep over, and I do not believe in the gross illusion of the Saint-Simonists,[4] for whom this "vale of tears" was to become a "paradise regained". The earthly paradise will not be met with again. Many promises of "happiness" and many over-grand programs are only swindles or childish dreams. Yet let us not relinquish any human hope of progress. Let us on the contrary work for all progress, with all our strength and on all fronts. But let us not be led into believing that progress ever reduces human evil, human tragedy: rather would it increase it. As he progressively escapes many of the tyrannies of his physical or social condition, man, finding himself in a position to know himself better and to pay

---

[4] The group of social idealists, inspired by the writings of Saint-Simon (1760–1825), who lived for a time in community at Ménilmontant under the leadership of Père Enfantin (1796–1864). The movement reached its apogee in the early 1830s, after which dissension among the organizers and the imprisonment of Père Enfantin led to its dispersion. Their search for a Woman Messiah who was to revolutionize the ethical basis of society and who was even sought by some Saint-Simonists in the Middle East marked the later stage of the movement. The failure to find her betokened its end.

more attention to himself, uncovers still further the drama of the human condition.

Besides, does not history show us that at many stages of civilization, by reason of the very progress made, the human conscience suffers an onslaught of pessimism, and is not the gravest temptation before which mankind marches the temptation of despair?

If you say that the development of the world is the development of mind, what place is there for the mind which observes and appraises this development?

If you justify all the sufferings and all the partial failures of this world by the consideration of the whole and of ultimate success, what is the worth of such optimism, which takes no account of the actors in the drama and which, in addition, does away with any spectator capable of making a whole of the show? Is this show-for-its-own-sake worth the sacrifice of everything to it? What is the worth of this new "theodicy" without souls and without God?

What enthusiasm is it hoped to arouse in us, or even what acquiescence is it hoped to gain, by explaining to us that we are the links in a great

chain?—in a chain which unrolls or seems to un-
roll only by crushing each of its links in turn?

None of the social constituents of pain goes below the surface. A lofty soul bears contempt,
insult, or slander easily enough. The only risk is
that it may transmute them into pride.

Egoism harbors pain and, at the same time, un-
selfishness amplifies it. The individual suffers
from the wrong that is done him, but the spirit
suffers still more in itself from the objective disor-
der that it perceives in this wrong.

"Jesus Christ will be in agony until the end of the
world." The sturdy lesson Pascal immediately
draws from this is common knowledge: "We
must not sleep during that time." But there is
another aspect of the Mystery of Jesus. There is
other fruit, nearer and sweeter. Until the end of
the world, Jesus will be in agony. Until the end of
the world, he will be nailed, with arms out-
stretched, on the cross. Whatever time it be, at

whatever moment of my life, I can always go to the Garden, to Calvary. I can really find Jesus there. I can shelter my agony under his; his laceration upholds my own. That naïve outburst of Peter's on the Mountain of the Transfiguration, that wish of his that could not be granted then and cannot be even now, can be voiced by me, when I come to Calvary or enter the Garden: "Lord, it is good for me to be here." And I am sure of never being repulsed.

Something will always be lacking to all suffering which has not been borne in solitude and secrecy. Even silence is not enough.

The vanity, the insipidity—worse than that, the falsity—of lives that are too successful. "The kingdom of heaven", said the Venerable Luis de la Puente,[5] "is the kingdom of the beheaded, the rejected, the afflicted, the scorned." There is no exception. Anything that would cast doubt on it

[5] The sixteenth-century Spanish Jesuit, who acquired a reputation for great piety. He was both writer and preacher (1534–1624).

is an optical illusion: really successful lives are always such only in retrospect. Or else, it is forgotten there are many ways, physical and moral, manifest or secret, of being "afflicted, rejected, scorned, beheaded".

"Blessed", says the Lord, "are the poor, those who hunger! Blessed are the persecuted!"

In the order of the spirit, a method of painless birth will never be found.

"Let us feed ourselves each day with pain and make ourselves ready, by today's suffering, to suffer tomorrow and the day after, and over and over again, until the time for change comes" (TASSO).

To what extent are we capable of suffering? To what extent have we the right, or perhaps the duty, to provide against suffering? To organize our lives against it? . . . Those are questions that call only for individual answers.

"All the suffering there is in this world is not the pain of agony, but that of parturition" (CLAUDEL). That is so, but in a certain order of things, the deepest, the most essential, it is agony itself which is parturition.

"Violaine, how you have suffered in the course of these eight years!

—Not in vain. Many things are consumed in the fire of a heart aflame."[6]

The evil which preys on our own selves is always the most unbearable. The ordeal which seizes hold of us is always the one among them all that we would have preferred to keep at bay. Each age, for the man who lives it and suffers from it, is always the worst.

[6] Paul Claudel, *L'Annonce faite à Marie,* Act iv, Scene 3.

It is a horrible thing to think that we are more anxious to know what the animal sufferings of our last moments will be, than to know if there is eternal life or to know if we shall be judged worthy of love or of hate. . . .

As the same fire liquefies certain substances whilst it solidifies others, so are there some souls that pain hardens, others whom it disintegrates.

Suffering is present everywhere. It must be respected everywhere, if it cannot everywhere be tended. One must first know how to divine it, but without affecting to see it.

Respect for man is composed mostly of respect for his suffering.

"Those who obtain something without trouble, keep it without love." (ST. THOMAS).

"But look thee here, boy. Now bless thyself: thou mettest with things dying, I with things new-born" (SHAKESPEARE, *The Winter's Tale,* Act iii, Scene 3).

Is joy to be found in progress—in discovery—or "in victory"? (JACOB BOEHME).

If it may be found in progress or discovery, it means that all real progress, all real discovery, is a victory over evil, over an obstacle, over a scandal, over some painful darkness.

When we say that evil has no positive reality, we are not saying that it is nothing, nor that it is only a lesser good, nor yet that it is only a shadow with no consistency, which is cast by the reality of good. We are not saying that it is only an indispensable constituent of universal harmony, and that it vanishes as an evil in the eyes of whoever rises high enough to perceive this harmony. We are saying on the contrary that it has all the terrible and sombre reality of *No*. It is not mere absence, but the antithesis of *Yes*. It is an antagonistic force, the pure power of negation, of refusal, of opposition, of revolt.

189

XIV

Interiority

The fear of prayer: is it fear of illusion, or fear of truth? Fear of psychological complications, or fear of God?

And is it not perhaps at the same time fear of finding one's self and fear of losing one's self?

Those who have never seen the sea believe that nothing is more monotonous—whereas nothing is more varied, nothing has more surprises in store.

The same is true of the inner life and of the contemplation of God. Without one's seeking presumptuously to "scrutinize Majesty", there is no end to the exploration of divine Immensity. No end to one's astonishment. You go from one discovery to another as you make your way in this infinite Simplicity. The wonders that come to light in it arouse ever fresh admiration.

"A vain subtlety": that is the term with which Bossuet opposed Malaval[1] in the same way as other mystics, because he had no understanding of the kind of contemplation that for them was a necessity. "A far-fetched metaphysics", which "throws our minds into unknown realms." The thing is of all time. Mystics are not the only victims of it. Those who have not had a certain sort of experience and have not themselves come up against obstacles of such a sort, are always ready to think that other people are inventing gratuitous refinements and complications for the sake of doing so.

There may be more things in a simple mystical feeling than in a long unfolding of thought. "Learned ignorance" has many ways of being—or of having been—"learned". Even the "emptiness"

---

[1] The blind seer of Marseille (1627–1710) was associated with Quietism and consequently opposed by Bossuet.

of the Buddhists is, as they say, a "fragrant emptiness", and this fragrance may resume in its own
way a whole scheme of human experience and
spiritual adventure. Not only the charm but the
strength of such as Fénelon lies in the way that a
long history of religion is condensed into a rare
essence in that "pure love" of his, where at the
same time a whole future takes shape.

Spiritual corpses stay dried up longer than temporal corpses before decomposing. But they are
none the less corpses.

This is the greatest corruption: to dissolve the
idea of good in the idea of usefulness; to dissociate
the means from the end, making them heterogeneous; to bring together on the same plane
(when not actually preferring the latter to the
former) homage to truth through the truthful
word and the tortuous act which will happily
result, so it is hoped, in the eventual establish-
ment of the reign of truth; to make us fall short of
the Gospel every day through the desire of making it fully effective some day.

The most tremendous hoax: the one that succeeds in persuading people that spiritual life is a hoax.

Many excellent people—right-thinking people of all sorts, prudent administrators, lovers of routine, friends of "order", decent citizens, men suspicious by nature, and so on—confuse spirit—all spirit, spirit itself, and even the Holy Spirit—with "bad spirit". That is what Aristophanes did, confusing Socrates with the Sophists. And what so many ecclesiastics did some time back, when they confused Newman with the liberals, that is to say, the modernists before their time. . . . For those who like the sort of solidity you can weigh, the kind of security you can establish, spirit is never a solid and certain reality. Spirit has no weight. It is never a force which gives you the feeling of being settled. It is a force which is ever free, ever inventive, and consequently ever disturbing.

If it is said: you believe in the beauty of spiritual life because you do not look at it close enough, then it may be asked if, when seen too near, the human face itself is really beautiful?

As if a certain optimum distance were not necessary to see what is true in human things!

All the ingredients of spiritual life may be impure. But spiritual life itself is an alchemy.

Much illusion enters into certain microscopic or underground ways of driving out illusion.

There are two well-established principles for keeping us ever courageous and content:

1. Anything worth doing always comes up against some obstacle. Anything taking effect provokes reaction. Only things that make no change in anything find their place under the sun without effort. Unanimous applause is always reserved for those who hold up an embellishing mirror to their public or who obligingly invest the public with their own voices.

2. The triumph of the spirit, like that of the humblest life, is the triumph of the improbable. It is normal for such a triumph to be rare and precarious. So we must always rejoice very much more at the least spiritual success than sorrow over the immense and grim extent of that conformism whose resistance to the life of the spirit is that of death itself. We must let ourselves be filled with wonder, as if it were a sheer miracle, by the

least green growth that defies the universal law of gravity. We must likewise be filled with wonder by the least growth of the spirit—even when it is not yet the Holy Spirit.

The dry heart's incapacity to love or the closed heart's determination not to are not signs of the heart's detachment. Distaste for prayer and spiritual things do not denote detachment with regard to the properties of the soul. Fear of battle and flight to a barren retreat do not indicate detachment with regard to the world. Detachment from human affections has its value only for the person who loves; detachment from spiritual preferences only for the seeker after God; detachment from action only for the man who fulfils his task like a man.

All spiritual teaching is based on ambiguity. It takes its stand of necessity on the experience of the senses, on customary notions, immediate desires, on the facts of ordinary daily life, in order to reveal a reality which is of quite a different order and to which there is no access through logic. All those things act as a springboard, rather than serve as a premise. We have to promote, not a horizontal progression, but a vertical movement, that very movement which of old was called "anagogy", and which nowadays we sometimes call "transcendence".

"I have come that they may have *Life*." "Whosoever drinketh of the *water* that I shall give him shall never thirst."

Now a wonderful thing happens, which is that there is a hidden complicity in us, a secret predisposition and a mysterious attraction, which makes the ambiguity effective, at least in certain cases. And the ambiguity is wholly justified after the event; or rather, once the *sursum* is accomplished, we understand that it was something other and more than an ambiguity. The passage to another order is not paralogism, because, for instance, *Life* is not, indeed, just a superior *life,* vaguely analogous to the one from which we started but with no real kinship with it; it is the fulness of life, in which all life is eminently contained; between all the realities indicated by this term *life* it establishes a symbolical relationship, in the original and radical sense of that word.

In the midst of so many discussions and inquiries about Christianity in our time, about its "lack of adaptability", about its "ineffectiveness", and so on—and properly conducted, such discussions and inquiries may be very useful, and may even be themselves a sign of vitality—there is, however, one very simple consideration which it would be a good thing to remember sometimes. It is that the best Christians, the most genuine and most living, are not necessarily or even generally counted among the learned or the clever; among the intellectuals or the politically-minded; among the custodians of power or wealth; among the "social authorities". Consequently, their voices rarely resound in the squares and in the press, their actions usually make no noise and do not take the public eye. Their lives are hidden from the sight of the world, and if they achieve a measure of fame, it is only rarely, in a restricted circle, or late in life. In the Church even, they often pass unperceived and the church-goer in critical mood will, in all good faith, fail to know them, though they may be by his side. Many saints are not known until after their death, and many, even after their death, remain unknown. Even those among them who had to play an important part in this world, were for the most part unappreciated, and, in their finest undertakings, either attacked or left in the lurch. It is nevertheless they who contribute more than anyone else to the difference that this earth of ours has from hell.

Now most of them hardly wonder, even today, if their faith is "adapted", or if it is "effective". They are content to live on their faith, which for them is reality itself, ever the reality of the actual moment, and the fruit that proceeds from their faith, though often hidden, is no less fine for that, nor less nourishing. Whatever be the state of the world, that fruit will always be needed to preserve some hope for us or give it back to us again.

"Such and such a person has a great fire in his soul and no one ever comes and warms himself by it, and passers-by see only a little smoke up above, coming out of the chimney, and then go on their way" (VINCENT VAN GOGH).

You are on the look-out for prophets. If these prophets whose rights you are always asserting and on whom you would almost like to see legal status and public recognition conferred, and even a license as well, really exist, they are indeed curious prophets. Never were there such, except false ones. Are you not afraid of encouraging the latter? Do you not think they are proliferating enough already? . . . When true prophets arise, remember that the safeguards normally tenable do not apply to them. Remember that they are spurned, slandered, humiliated; they are men accused of all the crimes against humanity; like Plato's just man, they are rejected and branded with the seal of infamy. Remember that these people stir everyone up against them, resisting popular passions just as they resist the whims of the great, preaching inopportune truths, telling no one what he wants to hear, breasting the tide alone, making mock of the ideas which turn our heads. . . . Remember that you yourself, if you met any, would not at first understand what they were saying; you would be tempted to hate them, to look them up and down contemptuously or to find them far too ill-timed; or else you would think they were in the service of your adversaries, or you would accuse them of stupidly playing their game—unless perhaps it were simpler still and you had great difficulty in perceiving them.

. . .And if you yourself thought one day you had heard the call which makes prophets of people, remember, moreover, that the road will be hard. After jibbing, when you are beaten at last, remember that you will have to do penance in sackcloth and ashes, blind yourself to all views of things which are purely natural, then inure yourself to affronts, beginning with the scorn of your nearest and dearest and the flight of your friends. . . .

We must not be over-surprised or complain un-
duly at staunch fighters not always being very
reasonable—nor at very reasonable people not always agreeing to become staunch fighters.

There are cases when one must say: "We must ask
God not only for spiritual graces, but for temporal ones as well": and other cases when one
must say: "We must ask not only for temporal
graces, but for spiritual ones as well."

Newman, in one of his sermons, refers to the
mystery which is as fully present in what we
think we know as in what we do not know at all;
and elsewhere he says that we do not discern the
presence of God when it is actually with us, but
afterwards, when we look back, at what is past
and concluded.

God has made us for Beatitude—and we meanly
look for happiness.

Happiness is what we conceive and desire

spontaneously. It is a thing unworthy of us, and which the deepest part of our nature rejects.

Beatitude is God.

The Christian does not ask for happiness. Jesus teaches him to ask for the Father's Name to be hallowed, for his Kingdom to come, for his Will to be done.

The Christian does not expect happiness. He expects the new heavens and the new earth, "which Justice inhabits".

The Christian does not desire happiness. He hungers and thirsts after Justice. He is athirst for eternal Life.

The Christian does not hope for happiness. He hopes to see the glory of God. *Satiabor cum apparuerit gloria tua.*[2]

. . .Happiness is all that and can be but that.

Spiritual studies (and spiritual life) are as inevitably put in false perspective when they allow the invasion of the unseeing science of psychology as

[2] "When thy glory dawns, I shall be well content", Psalm xvi, 15 (Knox).

are religious studies (and religious life itself) when they allow the invasion of the unseeing science of historical criticism.

These sciences are unseeing, not in their own sphere, but in the order of things which is not really theirs. To acknowledge this fact is in no wise to say that we must not utilize both of them and develop them thoroughly in their own particular order. There must be no timid psychology, no half-criticism! But we must recognize the fact that it is in any case difficult in practice for the same man to give these sciences the place due to them without yielding to that illusion which gives them all the place there is.

No spiritual impulse can resist that corrosive instrument which a certain sort of psychology constitutes.

But why deny what you kill?

All human activity must obey a twofold law and develop according to a twofold movement. Its necessary rhythm involves differentiation and unification, objectification and interiorization. Lacking the movement towards differentiation and objectification, moral life would remain in the clouds, neither sincere nor effective, vanishing into fine feelings and getting lost in abstractions; it would not really be *applied*. Lacking the inverse movement back to interiority and unity, it would become extrinsic, formalistic, dehumanizing; it would then be excessively codified; in the very perfection of its practice, it would not become accessible to the Gospel precept: "Be perfect as your heavenly Father is perfect."

Each man has different and precise duties, according to his station, his function, his responsibilities; the problems he has to solve day by day are not his grandfather's nor his neighbor's. But every man is also the same in his essence; he is the same before God; the same, too, before man.

There is no abstract morality, and that is why morality must specialize. But in what concerns spirituality, the worst abstraction would be to let one's spiritual self be diversified according to the conditions of the outer man. In its aim, in its impulse, in its essential laws, spirituality is one, or it is not at all.

Both things are expected of us: that we "recover the sense of the sacred" and that we "re-integrate the sacred into our everyday existence". But these are two opposed strivings, even though all of reality can and should be sacralized, even though the universe as a whole has a holy goal and even though Jesus' resurrection is for the universe a promise of its own resurrection in God.

Not everything, however, is sacred from its nature, so to say. If the holy were everywhere it would soon be nowhere, or it would become a very ambiguous "sacred" that one would be more justified in fleeing from than in "recovering".

Every man has different predetermined tasks, according to his milieu, his function and his responsibility; the questions which he must daily resolve are not those of his grandfather or his neighbor. But every man is also essentially the same: the same before God and also the same before other men.

No morality is abstract, and this is why it must specialize. But for the life of the spirit the worst abstraction would be to let oneself be squandered according to the conditions of the exterior man. In its true perspective, taken in man's total context, in its fundamental principles, the life of the spirit is always one and the same, otherwise it would be nothing at all.

As man has domesticated certain animals, so does society constantly undertake the domestication of the spirit. In all ages it has met with many successes in this art, both numerous and lasting.

Now it is this domesticated spirit, this "reflection", that Marxist theory, through too gross a confusion, is concerned alone to know. This theory refuses to see significant cases, which are always exceptional. It closes its eyes to the gushing forth of the spirit as well as to its perpetual overthrowing. It remains deaf, in fact, to all its explosions.

Is inwardness a luxury reserved for a few rare individuals, freed from all real worry? For those "whom God has sheltered", as Montaigne says, "from natural and pressing necessities"? For a Kierkegaard, with his private income and his good living? For a Bossuet or a Fénelon, very well off (though each behaving very differently) in domestic amenities? For a few monks who are poor but relieved of all burdens? And is it not a fact that what seems most genuine in the life of the spirit is, in that way, affected by a delusion more subtle than any "social delusion"?

There is an answer to that. As a rule there is a

way of telling the fake from the genuine and of recognizing not only the legitimacy but the necessity of the latter. Only, it is on condition that, when this question is raised, the person in whom it has been raised does not brush it aside as one waves away a troublesome fly.

Shall we leave the things of eternity, nobility of soul, the drama of inner life, and even God himself, in the hands of "prophets of the past"? Shall we let them be treated as things that are dead? Shall we leave ourselves open to the suspicion that we are indifferent to them? Shall we accept the declaration of a divorce between impulse and loyalty? Or between love of man and the service of God?

If we are right without prayer, if we are right without charity, if we are right without the Gospel, our "being right" is not only barren; it bears fruit of death. It is too easy to be right to the detriment of whoever is not, in thought or deed, complete perfection. Sometimes it is too tempting.

The evangelical is the boldest of all men; his boldness is ever fresh, always at his disposal, because he is independent and because his eyes discern all the warping and rotting which are for ever giving rise to falsehood, as soon as the first signs appear.

"The Truth shall make you free."

May the most loyal be the most bold! May such a man understand that loyalty always has need of boldness to be complete!

May the most bold be also the most loyal! May such a man understand that boldness always has need of loyalty, to be upright! May his boldness even be inspired in him by a stricter, deeper and more pressing loyalty!

The great mystics share in the privilege of the great classics of every order: their most individual teaching has a universal range, and at the very moment when their thought seems to be becoming abstruse and having a most rare case in view, it is still—in fact, more than ever—meat for all. All spiritual life, even the most elementary, can benefit from their lessons.

Take, for instance, the opinion of St. John of the Cross about the indifference one must have

208

with respect to "supernatural perceptions", even when the soul is certain that these perceptions come from God. It is both easy and fruitful to transpose this notion to several different domains. First of all, it is a lesson for every life of prayer: you learn in this way—and the humblest soul needs this training—to break yourself away from preferences that are too much a matter of feeling, not to take pleasure in easy piety, to distinguish the real reaching of God through faith, hope and love, from the whole psychological context which goes with it or sometimes counterfeits it. "The soul which takes its pleasure in the sweetness of a piety fed by feeling will never rise to the strong delights of the spirit." The same opinion still eminently holds good for intellectuals. It will help them not to take their attachment to their own conceptions for the love of God and not to take a heady excitement resulting from fine ideas for enthusiasm in the service of God; it will teach them what true knowledge is, the only real knowledge: faith that is naked, stripped, dark; it will put out their artificial lighting; it will save them from the misfortune lying in wait for them: that of embracing when they think they possess God, merely the products of their own minds, and of remaining for ever shut in themselves. . . .

All Christianity is like that; free from esotericism, but possessing several levels of meaning, all of which are in communication with one another; available to the most humble people in its very essence and not in some symbolic substitute; of inexhaustible substance for the most enlightened as for the most spiritual of men. The Sermon on the Mount was addressed by Jesus to the Twelve only, it was not teaching meant for the multitude, and yet it was thoroughly right of the Church to regard it from the start as having universal significance.

The unity of our faith, of our Christian spirituality, is restored to its original strength in each one of us, at all times, by drawing nourishment from the purest sap, which is hidden in remote sources.

"Ah! if only I met with life in your hearts!" (HASAN BOSRI).

"Always having as it were a morning freshness in the evening" (MAURICE BLONDEL).

"It is much better to die in the desert than serve the Egyptians" (ORIGEN, *Homily on Exodus v.4*).

❖

Read recently in a well-intentioned paper this appraisal of a film: "Here the drama is not social but intimate, and because of that less poignant, since melodrama triumphs over tragedy."

So all intimate drama is melodrama, and the only tragedy is social tragedy. Nothing which involves inner life alone is really "poignant". And I am well aware that the inner life of the film will only be a caricature; but why limit ourselves to that? And if you say: It is the testimony of an age of common-place socialization, then we may reply that fully human values will take their revenge all the more forcefully. Inner life may seem stifled by social life, as private life is by public life; but it is not dead. We must not despair of man.

XV

Faith

"Even if I shut my eyes, that would not destroy the sun."

Only, every one of us, almost always, shuts his eyes, keeps them shut, and in this persistent refusal we persist in believing that we have them wide open. And we are shocked at not seeing what we prevent ourselves from seeing.

When God becomes far off, problematical, unreal, perhaps it is salutary for us to use our imagination to extend the effect of this impression to the utmost; then perhaps the world, without God, will in its turn appear so unreal to us that the situation will reverse itself.

My light is only darkness. I cannot even say, by way of paradox, that it is luminous night. Yet its darkness discriminates better than any light. From all light unfriendly to it, from all false light, it turns me aside, *in full illumination*.

> "O night which is my guide
> More surely than the light of noon!"[1]

We do not want a mysterious God. Neither do we want a God who is Some One. Nothing is more feared than this mystery of the God who is Some One.

We would rather not be some one ourselves, than meet that Some One!

[1] This is an adaptation of some verses from the poem, *Noche Escura del Alma,* of St. John of the Cross:

> *Aquesta me guiaba*
> *Más cierto que la luz de medio dia. . . .*
> *¡Oh noche, que guiaste,*
> *Oh noche amable màs que el alborada. . . .*

❧

"How can I present Christianity, you say?"—
There is only one answer: as you see it.

"How can I present Christ?"—As you love
him.

"How can I talk of faith?"—According to what
it is for you.

There is in questions of this sort, when they
encroach too far, not a positive duplicity, no
doubt, but at least artifice, a lack of sincerity;
because there is a lack of faith.

❧

Christianity, it is said, owes this, that and the
other to Judaism. It has borrowed this, that and
the other from Hellenism. Or from Essenism.
Everything in it is mortgaged from birth. . . .

Are people naïve enough to believe, before
making a detailed study, that the supernatural
excludes the possession of any earthly roots and
any human origin? So they open their eyes and
thereby shut them to what is essential, or, to put
it better, to everything: whence has Christianity
borrowed Jesus Christ?

Now, in Jesus Christ, "all things are made
new".

Faith—if indeed it needs any support—will often rest better on reason that resists it than on reason that appeals to it.

In fact, in the depths of this same reason, and whatever the truth is about reasons for believing, appeal and resistance remain intimately coupled. Both of them equally characterize the creature in confrontation with God. Both are equally necessary, if it be true that faith is a fulness, and if it be true that it is a victory.

Is it the Father's Garden we yearn for, or simply the warmth of the maternal breast?

Religions—and many of their modern substitutes—tend to give us back that warmth. To remedy our growing old, they bring us back to our first childhood, indeed to our prenatal period. The time they restore to us is that before our history.

Christianity, however, lets us back into the Garden. Through it we triumph over time, not by denying time or going backwards, but by giving it all its meaning. Through it we share once more, not only in the youth of the world, but in the Youth of the Eternal.

Very many people honestly imagine they have critically penetrated to the very bottom of things, and they then proceed to offer us a faith which has far worse foundations and is far less coherent than the one they had just been criticizing. Instead of deepening it and perhaps improving it—something they could have done by listening to the great Catholic tradition, of which they are ignorant—they have taken "faith" as they found it within themselves and then judged it to be incorrigible. They have regarded this feeble possession as being a "literal interpretation of dogma". Consequently, any reflection about faith necessarily brought them further away from its true object and erected a new objection against their faith.

It seems that each of the great protagonists of contemporary atheism makes it a point of honor to prove that with him, from him onwards, now for the first time, as it were, mankind has progressed beyond the narrow perspective of antitheism; that in him it has at last become free; that henceforth, thanks to him, the idea of God can be envisaged without resentment, for resentment might give rise to suspicion as to the value of this denial of him; that the question of God will not even be posed in future; that belief in God, then, will no longer have to be fought; that the illusion will be dispelled for ever; that to our children's children he will be known only as a curio of the past. Such was the line taken by Comte and Marx; and, more recently, by Sartre and a few others. Each one outdoes his predecessor and, if he recognize any predecessors, it is he, so he thinks, who definitely opens the new era, by saying the last word on the subject.

But at the same time, the thought of God obsesses them, and the care even that they take to say they are going to deliver the human race from him once for all is a sign of this obsession, which is ever reborn. Nothing is more fiercely polemical, more anti-theist, more calculated to awaken the suspicion of resentment, than certain of their manifestos. Each of them wishes to prove, better than his forerunners, that unlike them he is at peace in his atheism and feels no need to think of God in order to "refute" him. But all that takes up a number of pages. And the concern that he shows in this way, producing a profusion of ever greater and greater subtleties and precautions, betrays him.

Criticism of what in Faith is inevitably impure can only be done from within and in the name of Faith. To be healthy, such criticism can only be a demand of Faith.

Any criticism which proceeded from a so-called flight of reconnaissance over unbelief and Faith, from a desire of mediation between one and the other, that is to say in practice from concession to unbelief, would be falsehood. It is Faith *as such* that calls for permanent, radical and *a priori* criticism of the idolatrous and superstitious elements with which our performance and our vital attitude are for ever encumbered. It is Faith *as such* which repudiates the fraudulent imitation and hypocrisy with which some people dishonor it. It is still Faith which of itself rises again, purifies itself, infuses vigor into itself in the souls of believers.

Does not atheism, you say, play a necessary role and even bring with it a positive value by fighting our Faith? I agree with you, in certain cases, at least, and my own experience bears this out. But

219

let me likewise think, at least, that Faith plays a necessary role and brings with it a positive value by opposing atheism. May your considerations not lead in one direction only. Do not compel me unilaterally to "understand" atheism instead of fighting it with the arms of the spirit.

To recognize that I am always more or less an unbeliever, to criticize the faults inherent in my belief, never to be satisfied with the present quality of my faith, to spurn all pharisaism both in faith and conduct: that is not to say that unbelief is partly right. It is to show it that it is wrong, as far as it depends on me, by my own behavior.

Very bold is the man who will decide at once whether such and such a way which becomes accessible to the spirit is the way of courage or of ease. Whether it is an heroic call or an evil temptation.

The most desperate solutions are not necessarily the most courageous.

There is a cowardly and silly fashion and there is an intelligent and courageous fashion of choosing both ways. An analogous mental giddiness may bring you down on either one side or the other. Therefore subjective considerations furnish no criterion. The choice must depend only on an objective examination and any scruple one way or the other must yield to an innocent love of Truth.

I am prepared to accept all of their science, but they—they cast all of my faith from their sight! How much better is my lot than theirs!

If you tell me: "All your beliefs in realities which you judge to be transcendent, belief in a God, in a Christ, in supernatural mysteries, in an eternal Kingdom, all that is only illusion", I can, without sharing this disillusioned and sad judgment, nevertheless understand it. It is like the horrible awakening from a too beautiful dream.

But if you tell me: "All that, which is so beautiful, was only symbolic; it was still a projection of the imagination, a figurative anticipation, a necessary stage in the development of the human mind or in the progress of earthly society, and we have now passed from the symbolic dream to the reality which is lived or at least thought", then, I ask to be shown that finer and more genuine reality! Let me be shown it in reality, or only in idea even! Is it not the prey which has been dropped for the shadow?

To reduce everything to obedience where faith is concerned may be a manner of saying that you do not care in the slightest about truth. And it is to be lacking thereby in the deepest kind of obedience, that of the spirit. No more in the domain of intelligence than of will does the spirit obey by surrendering. It does not offer the sacrifice of faith by putting "respectfully on one side" a store of dead dogmas which it forgoes discussing, but from which, on the other hand, it receives no inspiration either.

"Most of the faithful", as Fénelon already noticed in his day, "are too careless and indifferent about religion to be capable of bothering to contradict it." Many of them, today as then, only have that "vague faith" "which is satisfied", said Gérard de Nerval,[2] "with a few external practices

[2] A writer of delicate romantic fancy, Nerval (1808–55) wrote both poetry and prose and also translated *Faust* to Goethe's satisfaction. His dream world ultimately encroached so far on his daily life that for a time he was confined to a home for the mentally disturbed. On the 26th January, 1855, he was found hanged.

and whose apathetic adhesion is more culpable perhaps than the impiousness of heresy."

Orthodoxy: the most necessary and the least adequate thing in the world. (I mean, from the point of view of faith, and in so far as faith itself is concerned.)

The resistance of dogmatic data to many of our hypotheses is an excellent thing for preventing our thought from being facile.

The total submission of the spirit to Revelation is a fertilizing submission, because it is submission to Mystery. But the total submission of the spirit to any human system whatever is a *sterilizing* submission. Through the former I accept the conditions which make a dilatation of my thought possible. Through the latter I deny the very conditions.

Even with an apologetical intention, the doctrinal conformity demanded by men and which rejects all supernatural revelation, should not be likened to the unanimity of the Catholic Faith.

When we began to philosophize, we did not yet know what reflection was.

Perhaps when we begin to theologize, we do not yet know what faith is; at least, everything that faith is, all the demands it involves for the very exercise of the life of the spirit.

The danger of all religious philosophy is that of taking itself for religion; that of gradually replacing divine faith by human reflection; that of coming down to the natural sphere when you think you are going deeper.

The danger of all edifying theology is that of becoming cerebral piety.

Professors of religion are always liable to transform Christianity into a religion of professors.

The Church is not a school. It is not an elementary school.

It is said: The Galileo affair did not stay the progress of science.

Very well; but it achieved for a long time its divorce from theology. If science has not suffered by it, or only a little, can the same be said of theology?

When the world makes its way into the Church itself, it is worse than just being the world. Of the world it has neither the greatness in its illusory glamor nor that sort of loyalty it has in mendacity, ill-nature and envy, which are taken for granted as being its law. When the ecclesiastical world is worldly, it is only the caricature of the world. It is the world, not only in greater mediocrity, but even in greater ugliness. Yet never does that world, even in the worst moments, completely triumph. How many secret little islands there always are, refreshing oases, genuine and pleasing splendors! What hidden wonders of the Spirit, such as the world does not know!

But we must always be afraid of making ourselves unworthy of perceiving them.

Religion is most often made to serve morality. But you have then, to say the least, a most incomplete religion. How many people seriously make morality serve religion? Then only is the latter restored to its dignity, without morality being abased. Then only does it escape a number of wretched objections.

If heretics no longer horrify us today, as they once did our forefathers, is it certain that it is because there is more charity in our hearts? Or would it not too often be, perhaps, without our daring to say so, because the bone of contention, that is to say, the very substance of our faith, no longer interests us? Men of too familiar and too passive a faith, perhaps for us dogmas are no longer the Mystery on which we live, the Mystery which is to be accomplished in us. Consequently, then, heresy no longer shocks us; at least, it no longer convulses us like something trying to tear the soul of our souls away from us. . . . And that is why we have no trouble in being kind to heretics, and no repugnance in rubbing shoulders with them.

In reality, bias against "heretics" is felt today just as it used to be. Many give way to it as much as their forefathers used to do. Only, they have turned it against political adversaries. Those are the only ones that horrify them. Those are the only ones with whom they refuse to mix. Sectarianism has only changed its object and taken other forms, because the vital interest has shifted. Should we dare to say that this shifting is progress?

It is not always charity, alas, which has grown greater, or which has become more enlightened: it is often faith, the taste for the things of eternity, which has grown less. Injustice and violence are still reigning; but they are now in the service of degraded passions.

When, through excess of zeal, there is a tendency to confuse dogma and theology, far less is it an undue magnification of theology that results from it, than a misappreciation, a sacrilegious minimization of dogma, which thereby becomes reduced to a system of more or less clear ideas.

Even when people accept the classic distinction between dogma and theology, they may still be the victims of an analogous illusion. Dogma is then considered as a sort of minimum, that is to say, what every believer is obliged strictly to believe; dogma would thus correspond, in the order of faith, to what are, for morality envisaged from the point of view of casuistry, certain major precepts: that to which we are bound under pain of mortal sin. What wretched legalism in the matter of faith!

The reality, considered in depth, is just the opposite. Though Dogma and theology are always intimately related and can never be separated, yet they are never entirely of the same stuff. Dogma is a vast domain which theology will never wholly exploit. There is always infinitely more in Dogma, considered in its concrete totality, that is to say, in the very Object of divine revelation, than in this "human science of revelation", in this product of analysis and rational elaboration which theology always is. The latter, in its very truth, will always—and all the more in that it will always be rationally formulated—be inadequate for Dogma; for it is indeed the explanation of it, but not the fulness. This weakness is congenital. True theology knows that. It does not confuse the orders.

Faith, if it be really faith, is always one, always entire. It envelops the totality of its object—even in those parts of it which have not yet been made plain, or in those aspects which have not yet been explored. The same cannot be said, that is clear, of theology.

The greatness of theology. But the unique transcendence of faith. The true theologian is glad of

this. He takes a humble pride in his title of believer, above which he places no other.

"Anyone wishing to follow reason alone would be
a confirmed lunatic in the opinion of the greater
part of the world" (PASCAL). Anyone wishing to
follow faith alone is liable to be a confirmed here-
tic for many people—so little do the standards of
judgment of many men, seemingly the most jeal-
ous of orthodoxy, partake of the order of faith.

Anyone wishing, in what concerns faith, to be
guided by faith alone, must in any case be prepared to walk alone.

But his solitude is only apparent. It is a solitude
filled with invisible presences. It is the painful
condition of the deepest and purest communion.

May we always see in our spiritual leaders what
by God's act they really are, fathers, and whose
function gives them wholly to all men! May we,
by our spirit of faith, by our behavior towards
them, by our submissive demands, help them to
be such, if need be, incite them to be such! May
we, while accustoming ourselves to asking of

them "counsel, consolation, spiritual guidance", accustom them, if necessary, to play the part of father themselves towards us! For they need us in this way just as we need them. Whoever disparages his pastors, or is discouraged from having recourse to them, before humbly making this effort, is doubly culpable in regard to them.

It is not only to the unbeliever or half-believer, not only to the uninformed follower, it is to the churchman and the theologian, it is to the most spiritual and thoughtful Catholic, it is to all of us, with no exceptions whatever, that the remark made by Abbé Vicart to Antoine Thibaut in *Les Thibaut*[3] is addressed: "The Catholic religion, my friend, believe me, is far, far more than it has ever yet been granted you to glimpse."

Is there in the depth of your heart a loving home for her who is the Spouse of the Spirit and the Mother of the Living? Are you firmly attached to her who alone has inherited the Promises? Are you ready to die for her, always

[3] The long novel by Roger Martin du Gard (b. 1881), the first volume of which was published in 1922 and the last in 1940. It reflects life in the years before the First World War, mainly through the vicissitudes of two brothers.

remembering that she has given you Jesus Christ? Then, if that is so, you may give free rein to your zeal. You may desire, propose and call for reforms. You may reprove, criticize. . . . Perhaps you will be clumsy, violent, extreme, even unjust. Perhaps, because you desire and seek the best, you will commit many errors. So I do not say you will always be right, but I am not seriously worried about you. Even your mistakes will be better than the loveless contentedness of the over-accustomed churchgoer.

It is St. Augustine who tells you (but you must understand it aright, and not persuade yourself that it can be understood too cheaply): *Ama, et fac quod vis.*

The passion of wanting to reform everything in the Church is for the most part in inverse proportion to supernatural life; that is the reason why authentic and beneficial reforms almost never begin with such passion.

Lord God, keep us from deciding that a religion has "come of age"! And keep us even more from having ourselves a "religion that has come of age"!

To have the right to repeat the invectives that Jesus used against pharisaism with the same boldness, we should, like him, have to have nothing of the Pharisee about us. Like him as well, we must run no risk of becoming pharisaical in the very act of uttering the invective.

Let each one put himself to the test and let God put him to the test. And then, if he must, let him speak.

When we dream of the worship of pure spirit, or of a pure Church of the Spirit, we do not see the threat with which this dream is fraught: instead of the spirit of the letter, having only a letter of the spirit.

The Church stands firm, in spite of us. She stands firm by virtue of a divine power. And nothing stands firm but her. We daily give occasion for new mistrust, new scorn, new resentment, new calumnies in her regard. And daily, by the power of the Spirit, such occasions are transformed into instruments through which the faith is purified.

We compromise the Church daily, we muddy her daily, and daily she escapes all compromise and all stain. And daily, in spite of it all, God continues to call us to go on serving in the Church. . . . And daily new chosen ones come forward who cut right through appearances with that pure first glance of faith and demand that she give life.

You may say: You paint the Church in fine colors, you behold it in its ideal form, such as it should be, such as God desires it to be—such as it is in your dreams. . . .

To which I answer: No. I depict it—far from well indeed—such as it is in its mystery, that is to say, in its most real reality—but as faith sees it. I do not deny the ills of various orders, the moral order or any other, which at all times have affected it, which affect it today in each one of us. Indeed, I affirm them, I proclaim them, I declare the paradox and scandal to which they give rise and which are inherent in its very constitution.

As for describing these ills in detail, exhibiting these wounds, that would contribute nothing to our knowledge of the mystery of the Church. That must be left, then, in so far as their particular task demands it, either to historians, to

233

deal with the past, or to preachers to deal with the present, if they think it useful, or to investigators, "sociologists" or other reformers. Much more should it be left to good spiritual advisers—they are not in the habit of shouting aloud in the main squares. Anything else would only be facile scandal-mongering and ill-considered criticism.

And then, the Church is all of us. So it is I as well. By what right should I leave myself out of the picture? Now, I have no desire to make a public confession.

I have been told that a young intelligent priest, full of good qualities, has left the Church and apostatized, declaring he was scandalized by "certain attitudes on the part of the hierarchy". I am not interested in what these "attitudes" were. I am willing to grant, as a hypothesis, with my eyes shut, that these "attitudes" were in fact regrettable. I am even willing to imagine worse ones. But what was this young priest's faith, then, before the disaster happened? What was his idea of the Church? What consciousness had he of the life he received from it and what esteem for it? And did he know so little of its history? One cannot wonder that his experience was brief; had he never read in his breviary the homily where St. Gregory explains that you must never expect to find a domain without scandals before the coming of the Kingdom? Young as he may still be, could he wonder himself at men sharing in the human condition? Or of what nature is the logic whose course he has followed?

Even should St. Paul, at the time of the conflict at Antioch, have had twenty times more to complain of than St. Peter, even should he have considered, rightly or wrongly, that the "attitude" adopted by the "pillars of the Church" was twenty times more scandalous, can it be imagined that his faith in Christ would have been the least bit shaken? Or that this scandal would have been capable of alienating him, however slightly, from the one Church of Christ? Our faith is the same today, the foundations are the same, it has been kindled at the same Hearth, the same Spirit continues to infuse it in our hearts—and it is always the same Church; which disappoints us and irritates us, which for ever makes us impatient and discouraged, through all those elements in her that are related to our own wretchedness, but which at the same time pursues its irreplaceable mission among us, which does not cease for a single day to give us Jesus Christ; in whom the Father "delivers us from the power of darkness

235

and transports us to the Kingdom of the Son of his love".

⚜

. . . *Quis nos separabit a fide et spe et caritate Christi?*[4]

---

[4] "Who will separate us from the faith and hope and the love of Christ", an elaboration of Romans vii, 37 *(Quis nos separabit a caritate Christi?)*.